Presented to:
PUMP SPRINGS MEDIA LIBRARY

Donor
Linda Weaver

The more I read and study about biblical characters, the more intrigued I become with their personal lives.

This is why I find Angela Ramage's book, *Windows to the Heart of God*, captivating reading. Like me, she has researched and investigated the lives of biblical personalities. But in a moving docudrama fashion, she portrays those biblical characters for us in a distinctively compelling manner. Your emotion, intellect, and will are engaged to comprehend and appropriate the principles of Scripture that are always behind the men and women of God's Word.

Angela Ramage is a woman with a heart for God. She writes for the most enduring of all reasons—to draw individuals into an intimate relationship with Christ.

Dr. Charles F. Stanley
Senior Pastor, First Baptist Church
Atlanta, Georgia

Windows to the Heart of God portrays imaginatively and powerfully seven "minor" characters forever changed by their encounter with Jesus during His earthly sojourn. More than that, the author shows that the Lord Jesus still longs to impact people today with that same healing love and total forgiveness. This work maintains a careful balance between biblical and doctrinal soundness, creative reflection, and contemporary application. Both those who wonder what it was like to meet Jesus "back then" and those who struggle with how to make real their daily relationship with Jesus "right now" will benefit greatly by reading *Windows to the Heart of God*.

Kendell H. Easley, Ph.D.
Associate Professor of New Testament and Greek
Mid-America Baptist Theological Seminary

I highly recommend the book by Angela Ramage, *Windows to The Heart of God*. Truly, one feels he is looking through those windows when he reads the beautiful descriptions of persons and events recorded in this book. Angela's use of descriptive words makes each event come alive, . . . and [her] inspirational thoughts following these events bring you closer to God. I can recommend it to every Christian, and to those who do not know Christ, it can be a vehicle by which they can see God in a new light.

Paul L. Alford
President, Toccoa Falls College

One of the greatest benefits to understanding and applying God's Word to our everyday lives is to be able to see the realness of the people and events of the Bible. In *Windows to the Heart of God*, Angela Ramage has helped us to see some people and events in Scripture in new and memorable ways. This book will touch your heart—and it will give you a new appreciation for the marvelous grace of God's heart.

Mary Whelchel
President and founder of the radio program
The Christian Working Woman

WINDOWS
TO THE
HEART
OF
GOD

ANGELA RAMAGE

Publishers Since 1798

THOMAS NELSON PUBLISHERS
Nashville • Atlanta • London • Vancouver

Published in Nashville, Tennessee, by Thomas Nelson, Inc., Publishers, and distributed in Canada by Word Communications, Ltd., Richmond, British Columbia, and in the United Kingdom by Word (UK), Ltd., Milton Keynes, England.

Unless otherwise noted, all Scripture quotations are from the NEW KING JAMES VERSION of the Bible, © 1979, 1980, 1982 by Thomas Nelson, Inc., Publishers.

Scripture quotations noted NIV are taken from the HOLY BIBLE, NEW INTERNATIONAL VERSION ®. Copyright © 1973, 1978, 1984 by International Bible Society. Used by permission of Zondervan Bible Publishing House. All Rights reserved.

The "NIV" and "New International Version" trademarks are registered in the United States Patent and Trademark Office by International Bible Society. Use of either trademark requires the permission of International Bible Society.

Library of Congress Cataloging-in-Publication Data

Ramage, Angela.
    Windows to the heart of God / Angela Ramage.
      p. cm.
    Includes bibliographical reference.
    ISBN 0-7852-7912-1 (alk. paper)
    1. Jesus Christ—Influence.   2. Jesus Christ—Friends and associates.
   3. Jesus Christ—Devotional literature. I. Title.
BT303.R36   1996
232—dc20   95-13224
                                              CIP

Printed in the United States of America

1 2 3 4 5 6 7 — 00 99 98 97 96

Dedicated to the loving memory of my grandmother,
Margaret Alzada Doster Allen—
until we meet again in His presence.

CONTENTS

FOREWORD

I have always been fascinated by the men and women of the Bible. In fact, much of my preaching has focused on the lives of biblical characters because I find people readily identify with their very human struggles and challenges.

The more I read and study about the biblical characters, the more intrigued I become with their personal lives. For instance, Genesis chapters 39 through 41 chronicle the amazing story of Joseph's slavery, imprisonment, and eventual rise to power. It is a concise presentation of thirteen hard years of Joseph's life. While the Scriptures record all we need to know for solid faith, I am sure there were many cold, lonely nights and difficult days that Joseph endured that are not recorded there. I wonder, did he not wrestle with feelings of rejection? Did not betrayals wound his spirit?

This is why I find Angie's book, *Windows to the Heart of God*, captivating reading. Like me, she has researched and investigated the lives of biblical personalities. But in a moving docudrama fashion, she portrays those biblical characters for us in a distinctively compelling manner. You can almost see the calloused knees of the prophetess Anna as she prays and waits for the promised Messiah; feel the amazement when the cynical Matthew encounters Christ; sense the power of Christ's healing touch on the woman with the issue of blood; see the love in Jesus' eyes for the thief on the cross. You will also marvel at Angie's insights into the lives of the Pharisees, Joseph and Nicodemus, the disciples on the road to Emmaus, and the young lad whose loaves and fish fed the throng gathered on the Palestinian hillside.

Pointed applications at the end of each chapter fasten you to the timeless truths that mark each character. Your emotion, intellect, and will are engaged to comprehend and appropriate the principles of Scripture that are always behind the men and women of God's Word.

Angela Ramage is a woman with a heart for God. She writes for the most enduring of all reasons—to draw individuals into an intimate relationship with Christ. Her editorial work at IN TOUCH MINISTRIES® through the years has always reflected this passion. May each of her stories endear you to the love Christ has for you and remind you of your very special worth to Him and to His Kingdom.

DR. CHARLES F. STANLEY
SENIOR PASTOR, FIRST BAPTIST CHURCH
ATLANTA, GEORGIA

ACKNOWLEDGMENTS

I'll never forget the first time I heard of God's faithfulness. I had accepted Jesus as my Savior on Wednesday, February 16, 1979. The following Sunday, I was in church hearing of God's unconditional love and grace. I remember wondering, *Can this really be true?*

I grew up hearing the stories of the Bible, but I never understood how they applied to my life. Once I was saved, questions filled my mind: Were the stories real? Did the people actually exist, and if so, what were their thoughts? How did they perceive Jesus? How did He feel about those He met? What was it like to know the Son of God during His earthly ministry? Could anyone ever be the same after meeting Him?

Amy Carmichael once wrote, "It was not what Jesus did that calmed the wind; it was Who He was." None of us is eternally changed by altering physical circumstances. The people of Jesus' day did not receive their sight or any other physical healing as a result of what Jesus did. It was contact with the presence of God that eternally changed them. So it is with us. Once we come in contact with the Savior, we are never the same.

Our world knows much heartache and suffering; a large amount is physical, but much more is emotional and mental. While we long for physical healing, the need is much greater for emotional and mental restoration. People need to know that God loves them, that He accepts them and has a plan for their lives (Jer. 29:11). Only Jesus has the power to calm the raging waves of insecurity, the hopelessness of divorce, the pain of rejection, the loneliness of death, and the heartache of terminal illness.

If you have ever suffered, then you know what it feels like to need someone to tell you that things will be OK. God is that kind of friend to each of us. *Windows to the Heart of God* provides an opportunity for us to step into the brightness of His love and eternal care. Each chapter represents a different aspect of His loving nature. I pray that as you read these pages your love for the Savior will be strengthened, refreshed, and renewed.

I am deeply grateful to Dr. Charles Stanley, who remains my teacher and pastor. Had it not been for his deep, abiding love for Jesus Christ and desire to teach me and countless others how to live the Spirit-filled life, I might never have discovered that living by faith is much more than something you hear at church on Sunday—it is a way of life.

I also would like to say a special thank you to Rev. Fred Lodge. While in college, I came to a point of crisis in my spiritual walk with God. Fred allowed God's unconditional love and acceptance to shine through him. My life was changed forever as I accepted God's unconditional acceptance of me. Much gratitude is given to my friend Pat

McGarvey whose constant prayers and encouragement often refreshed me during times of difficulty and doubt (2 Tim. 1:16). My thanks also go to those at IN TOUCH MINISTRIES® who have faithfully read and reread my manuscript. Their prayers and encouragement have offered much hope and incentive. Nothing in life is complete without the love and support of family and friends—Mom, Dad, Jay, Tracy, and Abigail—thanks for believing in me. I would also like to thank Rick Nash at Thomas Nelson for his guidance and encouragement.

Above everything, I am eternally grateful to my Lord and Savior, Jesus Christ, for allowing *Windows* to be printed. Whenever I reread this manuscript I often catch myself wondering, *Who wrote this? I don't recognize these words.* It's not because I didn't type the letters and hit the space bar, it's because this is His story, not mine. I could never create such images of love, forgiveness, compassion, and hope. Nor could I ever bring such truth to life. God is the author—to Him be eternal glory and praise.

ANGELA RAMAGE
ATLANTA, 1995

CHAPTER 1

Window of Promise—*Anna's Song*

A single, aging voice made its way upward through the cool, damp grayness of the temple walls until it touched the edge of heaven's gate. In eighty-five years, it had never once passed unnoticed. Now, all of heaven broke forth in swift alertness at its arrival.

Today was the chosen day for the answer to be revealed, and all of heaven was ablaze with the news. The swing of the pendulum, which began forty days before with the birth of a tiny baby, roared past the scale of human time with one giant sweep as the Light of God drew near to this one thin, frail moment in time.

"I lift up my eyes to You, O God. Only You can redeem Your people. Only You can bring Messiah. My days are in Your hands and though I am old, I wait for Your redemption with a young heart. Though my eyes have grown dim, when He comes I know I will see His face. For Your promises are true, O Lord, my God. You are faithful. Messiah will come to Israel and walk among His people. May Your servant ever be blessed by the knowledge of His coming, even today."

Anna was silent for a moment. Then slightly adjusting the

cloth that covered her head, she looked up through the sunlight now filtering through the temple. The holy presence of God moved around her. She recognized its coming the moment the last words had crossed her lips.

Morning prayers usually stretched into the afternoon, but for some reason there was a strange completeness to her thoughts and words. Something she had never felt before. There was nothing more she could add, no other petition to be lifted.

A residing peace filled her heart as she lowered her head in wonder of God's faithfulness. Had her friends Miriam and Sarah been present, they would have seen the glow of God on her face, but they had not yet arrived. So there in the quietness of the new day, Anna enjoyed the warmth of God's nearness.

Then bending to the left, she lifted herself from the stone floor. There were times when her knees wanted to refuse the weight of her body. However, the numbness of her joints and the pain associated with age never kept her from prayer. Daily she raised her outstretched hands in hungry expectation to God for an answer to her request. Her prayers were always filled with an inviting newness. They spoke of the wisdom of God, so much so that she was called a prophetess.

The three things wisdom had taught her over the years were patience, endurance, and persistence. She knew that God had called her to a life unlike those of other women. Her husband had died when she was still young enough to bear children, to dream, and to see her dreams become a reality. Some might think her dreams died along with her husband, Joel, but this was not so of Anna.

She waited, waited in the knowledge and grace that few before her had known. She waited in the seasoned love of her God, in the faithfulness of His promises, and in the hope of prophecy being fulfilled within her lifetime. She waited even when disillusionment chased her mind with thoughts of fear and abandonment. She waited, often alone in the temple, within the confines of the tiny room provided for her. She waited long after the others had gone and the candles of the day were all blown out. Often, there in the darkness of the temple, with only the light from the Holy of Holies filtering out and across the stone floor, Anna would cry silently as she renewed her hope in the promises of God.

Today, God would lift the veil of time and cross an earthly courtyard in answer to her prayers. However, as yet, Anna was unaware of His coming.

For the moment, her mind was drawn to her aging hands. They seemed much older to her this morning. The coolness of the temple had stiffened them. Her knees shuddered at the sudden shift in weight as she rose to her feet. They, too, bore the marks of a prayer warrior, heavily calloused from years of kneeling on her prayer mat.

Human eyes seldom noticed these wounds of time and age—only God and Anna knew, and yet, she valued every ache, every pain, as heavenly commendations of fulfillment of God's plan for her life. She had been chosen as His instrument of prayer.

I guess I'm finally getting old. She smiled to herself as she looked up at the temple's walls. A sharp reminder of God's promises swept through her mind—promises she had carried in her heart for years, ones that she believed would bring Messiah to these very porticoes.

A flock of doves gathered in one of the top corners of the stone structure. Stretching their wings, they jolted into flight without warning, and Anna turned in their direction. Had something frightened them? She saw nothing; only the prayers of a few women echoed through the court.

A lone, white dove balanced along a stone ledge. *A rascal,* thought Anna, smiling. *You probably escaped from the cage of a temple merchant.*

Herod had built this temple as a gesture of goodwill to the Jews. Anna scoffed at the notion. There were parts of it that were still under construction. Stones weighing several tons formed its walls. Yet, even in all its splendor and strength, it was spiritually broken.

Beggars lined its steps, and merchants openly sold animals on its main porch. Even the sacrifices offered were tainted by complacency and obligation. Religious leaders were shrouded in political unrest.

Anna had learned at an early age that it was her worship, love, and prayers that God desired and not an inspiring political viewpoint. When her husband died, she left her home and committed her life to praying and waiting for the coming of Messiah. It was not just a personal desire—both she and her husband knew Messiah's coming was near.

The Spirit of God had drawn her to the temple. And even now at 104, His call to her was just as real, just as fresh as it was the first day she experienced it.

The small flock of doves was now circling the ceiling. They

4

seemed nervous, even agitated, but a closer look changed her mind. Their flight had all the telltale signs of a celebration. Periodically, one or two landed on one of the ledges for a moment before joining back with the group.

From where Anna stood, the Beautiful Gate was in full view, and for some strange reason she was instinctively drawn to it. A chill of excitement swept over her as she crossed the stone pavement.

"He will come one day," Anna whispered, "to this very spot. Messiah will walk on these stones—the same ones I am now standing upon."

A heartwrenching thought raced through her mind. She had felt it before, but she had fought its entrance. This time she knew its messenger was from God.

He will come, though they will know Him not.

Quietly she lowered her head. *Oh, Jehovah, how . . . how could Your own people not know You?* A tear traced her wrinkled face and clung to her lower cheek. The time for questions such as this was not yet at hand.

A stirring of wings once again disrupted her thoughts. She looked up, but the doves were gone. A coolness blew past her as the streaks of morning sunlight blazed across the temple floor.

Anna's eyes caught a quick glimpse of Simeon moving hurriedly through the shadows of the columns and out through the women's court. He too had waited years for the coming of Messiah and believed God's redemption was truly at hand. She could not imagine where he was going at such a swift pace. The urge to follow him was overwhelming.

5

She almost called out, but Simeon was gone, disappearing beyond the walls of the court and out onto the porch area. She was winded by the time she reached the massive columns that surrounded the structure. Wondering if she had the strength to continue, she turned and saw, a few yards in front of her, Simeon and a young couple.

Such youth, was her first thought as her eyes met those of the young woman at her husband's side. Their youthfulness seemed to light up the entire area surrounding them. Wonder filled her eyes as she returned her gaze to elderly Simeon.

His back had been to Anna, and as she approached them she realized Simeon was weeping.

"Simeon," whispered Anna.

He turned in her direction, and as he did, Anna's heart was taken aback. Simeon was holding a child. His face was wet with tears of joy and his eyes begged her to draw near.

"The promise, Anna!" His voice shook then strengthened. "The promise God gave to Israel is here!" And lifting the child slightly up into the cool of the morning air, Simeon blessed God. "Lord, now Your servant can die in peace. For I have seen Your promise with my own eyes! I am holding Your salvation. Truly He will be a light of revelation to the people and the glory of Your people Israel!"

His words broke off as he pulled the baby back to his chest and turned to the mother. Almost sorrowfully he said to her, "A sword shall pierce your soul, for this child shall be rejected by many in Israel, and this to their undoing. But He will be the greatest of joy to many others. And the deepest thoughts of many hearts shall be revealed."

His mother's eyes deepened and pooled over with tears as her husband drew her tightly to his side. Neither understood what these aging saints knew. God was now among them—eternity had come this day.

Anna softly lifted the cloth away from the baby's head and cheeks. His skin, still reddish in color, was filled with the newness of life. Instinctively, His tiny hand unfolded and reached to meet Anna's probing fingers.

Eternal love reaching out to a common, widowed woman. God had answered the deepest desire of her heart—her prayers had been heard.

Slowly Simeon lifted the child and, with an approving nod from His mother, placed Him in familiar arms. Arms that for years had been bent in faithful prayer for His coming. Arms that had withstood hours of being lifted to heaven in petition for Israel and its redemption.

Hands and fingers that He had witnessed so often folded in prayer now caressed His face and supported His head. And in the brightness of the morning's light, the Son of God squinted as He tried to focus His earthly eyes on one so fair and lovely in His sight.

This was one of salvation's finest moments. Nestled in the outer folds of Anna's prayer cloth, Jesus viewed His beloved servant, and for those few moments no heart, human or eternal, knew more joy than hers.

A WINDOW TO GOD'S HEART

In our world of instant answers, many find it hard to imagine how a prayerful, temple widow could remain faithful in her belief, day after day, year after year, with little to no response from God; but Anna did just that. Her faith weathered years of silence when from a human perspective it appeared God had forgotten His people. And when God did speak to her heart, she treasured His promise and proclaimed its coming.

We can only imagine the joy she felt as she saw Jesus for the first time. God had answered her prayers—her eyes beheld the Messiah, the fulfillment of the promise to Israel and mankind.

There are no small prayers in God's eyes. He values each word we speak to Him along with every thought, every heartache, every tear, every moment of laughter and joy. So never think for a moment that your prayers go unnoticed by God. He hears every prayer, even the ones too difficult for human expression.

However, God has a timetable. He knows the precise moment to answer our requests. Anna prayed for years with expectation. Her hopes were not dashed. In God's timing, He came to her and He will come to you.

Perhaps you are facing a time of discouragement or defeat. You have clung to the promises of God for weeks, months, or even years. Now, in frustration, you find yourself being tempted to yield to doubt, walk away from what you know is true, and forget it all. Take courage. God is near and He will complete the work He has begun in you (Phil. 1:6).

More than likely, Anna was tempted more than once to give up her vigil. Yet God gave her a promise and she believed He would bring it to pass. Luke tells us "She never left the temple but worshiped night and day, fasting and praying" (Luke 2:37 NIV).

Three words always come into play whenever we place our trust in God for a specific promise: *focus, steadfastness,* and *expectation.*

Set your focus on Jesus Christ.

Four hundred years of prophetic silence separated the faith of Anna and the prophets of old. Yet she received God's promise into the depths of her heart and in believing faith prayed that He would send His redemption to His people. Her focus was not on the darkness that surrounded her—the political unrest and religious piety of her society were of no concern to her. She was focused on God and His ability to redeem all who placed their trust in Him.

What is in your life that is in need of a touch from the Savior? Believe that when you pray, God hears you. He is not a distant God but is ever near to you. And if you will call to Him, He will answer.

Be steadfast in your prayers.

Anna did not run from person to person in an attempt to confirm the promise God gave to her. Instead she remained devoted to God and served Him daily in the temple. Warren Wiersbe writes in *The Bible Exposition Commentary*, "Widows didn't have an easy time in that day; often they were neglected and exploited in spite of the commandment of the Law."†

None of us are immune to doubts and fears. The problem

9

is not that they appear, but what you do with them when they do come. Are you tempted to give up, toss in the towel, and walk away? Anna had one thought—God's coming redemption—and she refused to be moved or defeated.

The next time you want to quit and walk away from something you know God has given you, stop and consider the faithfulness of God. Ask Him to give you a specific verse of Scripture concerning your situation. Then when doubts come you can turn to that passage and claim the promise of His victory.

Expect God's promise.

God's timing is always perfect. And Anna's joy is reflective of this. For years, she waited in hopeful expectation for God's redemption to appear. When she approached Mary and Joseph and a tearful Simeon, she knew God's promise of redemption was complete. There within Simeon's arms was the Son of God. One of the sidebars to a believing faith is learning to live in the expectation of what God will do if you will trust Him. Anna believed God when others doubted. She remained in the temple, despite the loneliness and isolation. She knew when Messiah did come, the first place He would appear would be the temple. And it was so.

Are you living in hopeful expectation of what God will do for you? God's window of promise to you is found in Jeremiah 29:11–13: "For I know the thoughts that I think toward you, says the LORD, thoughts of peace and not of evil, to give you a future and a hope. Then you will call upon Me and go and pray to Me, and I will listen to you. And you will seek Me and find Me, when you search for Me with all your heart."

Jesus is the God of all hope and restoration. No matter what you have faced in the past, He will heal your hurts, bring peace to your soul, and give you a future if you will come to Him.

† Warren Wiersbe, *The Bible Exposition Commentary* (Wheaton, IL: Victor Books, 1989), 178.

CHAPTER 2

Window of Calling—*The Gift of God*

He was late. The sun was up and the city streets were already filling with people. Hurrying along, Levi's eyes caught sight of a young, Jewish man standing near a market cart. *He owes me two months in back taxes,* thought Levi. *I should have him thrown in debtor's prison, but then I never would see the money.*

Instead of stopping, Levi picked up his pace and headed for the waterfront. He was a publican, though in some circles he was referred to as a tax collector. He preferred the formal title. It suited him better, he thought, and softened his image. He worried about his position, or rather the lack of it. Yet his concern was not enough to keep him from advancing his financial future.

"Rome needs good men like me," he often boasted. "Taxes must be collected one way or the other. At least with me, the people pay another Jew and not a Roman thief."

Yet greed was Levi's motivator. It was not uncommon to find him charging far above the required amount. He padded his wealth while Rome turned its back to his deeds. To them it was a joke, brother stealing from brother. In fact, the Jews were a joke to the Roman government, but they were also a force that could not be taken too lightly.

Levi was right. He was needed by the government. He grew up in Capernaum and knew the names and the faces of most of those who lived there. However, his occupation had its drawbacks—isolation, for one. None of his childhood friends would give him the time of day. The only solace he received was from others of his profession and a few members from the lower ranks of the Roman hierarchy.

As he turned the corner and headed down the hill that overlooked the Sea of Galilee, his eyes scanned the harbor. It was a beautiful scene. The deep blues of Galilee contrasted with the sun-bleached shoreline. Fishing boats dotted the horizon as merchants and traders busied themselves peddling their goods on the docks.

The sea and the activity of the shoreline never failed to excite him. He remembered the evenings when, as a child, he hid among the docked boats. Crawling inside an unsuspecting bow, he would lie back and watch as the stars nodded and blinked to one another. "God's candles to all mankind," Levi would whisper.

He often thought back to those times and wondered how his life could have changed so much. What had happened to his childhood dreams? What had changed his love for Jehovah?

It must be the way life is. We grow up and things change. Not even God can remain the same forever. He vowed never to disclose to anyone his doubts and fears concerning the Lord. *Religion is a private matter—something between a*

*person and God—not something for every priest or pious Jew
to know and scrutinize.*

"Watch where you are going!" came a shout immediately
in front of him. Levi's daydreaming had led him directly in
the path of a crippled, old man. Before he could stop himself,
Levi had stumbled over the old man and sent him angling to
the ground.

Squinting through the sunlight, a look of recognition
passed over the old man's face. When Levi reached to help
him to his feet, the old man recoiled in anger. "I suppose all
you were thinking of was yourself and your money! Too busy
to watch where you are going! Too mighty to even care!"

Holding up two fingers and rubbing them together in Levi's
face, he continued his assault. "You care nothing for the poor.
May God curse you and your whole household!" With that he
struggled to his feet and disappeared into the crowd that had
gathered.

Levi was stunned and for a moment said nothing. Finally,
he retorted, "Broken old man, who asked for your opinion?"
With that he turned and walked a few yards to the double doors
of his office.

In order to leave the port area, merchants and fishermen
had to pass Levi's place of business. Often he would do
business from a wooden table just outside the doorway of his
office. When business was brisk, as he hoped it would be
today, being near the street made it easy for him to detect those
who were trying to leave the area without paying taxes.

However, fishing had been slow recently. For several days
now, the men had fished throughout the night and caught

nothing. One fisherman named Simon, also called Peter, was a leader among the men in the harbor. For three days Simon had fished the waters of Galilee and caught nothing. Levi knew Simon as a boy and, like many others, Simon owed him money. The poor fishing was a bad sign for Levi's business.

Levi was always amazed by his own generosity. He recently had granted an extension to the fishermen, including Simon, until business picked up. Yet, despite the gesture, Simon thought Levi was a lying thief, and Levi thought Simon was nothing more than an abrasive, belligerent fisherman with an uncontrollable mouth.

"I have never seen anything like this," Levi said to his assistant Daniel as he entered his office.

"Like what?"

"There must be close to twenty boats out on Galilee, even though the sun is high in the sky. Have they not caught anything?"

"I don't know," mused Daniel. "Word on the street is 'no', and they will be coming in soon."

"It's too much work for me. I don't see how they can keep throwing the nets out time after time."

"They know they owe you money, Levi. And it drives them to try just once more before giving up."

"That's true." Levi nodded as he glanced back out the door and down to the water. "Well, it looks as though some of them are coming in. Let's get the table outside. It won't be long before we see what, if anything, they caught."

Levi stepped back to the doorway and called to a young boy standing across the street.

"Nicholas!" Levi shouted.

He often used the boy as a "runner" or a spy. Nicholas was young and agile and without much effort could get in and out of the tightest of spaces. This was a welcomed quality along the packed and hurried streets of Capernaum.

Many of the fishermen tried to conceal their total catch so they would be charged a smaller tax. If Rome noticed a decline in the levied taxes, Levi would be held responsible.

There was also a growing sense of rebellion among the merchants and fishermen. They had grown weary of the heavy taxes, and Levi feared a revolt against him. Not only could this cost him his Roman position, it could cost him his life!

"Nicholas, come quickly!" shouted Levi.

Leaving his friends, Nicholas hesitated before slowly crossing the street.

"Today you will send me back to the fishermen, but there will be nothing to report," he said, looking slightly irritated.

"What do you know?" Levi bristled. "Have you been down to the waterfront this morning? Or better yet, have you ever turned down one of my shiny coins for your trouble?"

"No."

"Nor will you today. Hurry along. I want to know what the catch is like. And, Nicholas, check on Simon; he owes me quite a lot in back taxes. I think it's time to demand a payment."

"Levi, there is nothing down there today except a Jewish teacher who is telling everyone the kingdom of God is at hand."

"So tell Him you are one of Israel's lost lambs and perhaps He will carry you on His shoulders," said Levi, laughing.

He, too, had heard of this teacher, as had most of Capernaum. But then there was always someone claiming to be something. Another Jewish teacher was nothing special.

Levi's eyes glanced down the street to where it ended near the water. A crowd of listeners gathered near the shoreline.

At least this One takes His message to the people. He sighed. Then he turned his attention to a heavy looking bundle on the back of a small donkey, the first collection of the day. "May it be profitable," Levi said while opening a wooden box containing weights and a list of the taxes to be levied.

By the time Nicholas reached the waterfront, the Jewish teacher was standing in the bow of a small fishing boat just off the shore. It was Simon's boat, and it was just as Nicholas had thought—no fish again today.

The people were everywhere, some listening, others passing or stopping out of curiosity.

He's a common looking man, thought Nicholas as he watched the Teacher continue His lesson. Then turning to a nearby servant girl he asked, "What's His name?"

"The people call Him Jesus. He's a teacher from Nazareth."

Jesus had finished speaking to the crowd and turned to say something to Simon.

A soft laughter rose from the fishermen. Two of the men standing near Nicholas laughed together. "Can you believe it? He wants Simon to put back out into deep water and drop his nets."

"He's a teacher, not a fisherman, Simon!" shouted one of the men.

Jesus faced Simon and looked out over the Sea of Galilee. Simon looked from Jesus to the questioning faces of his friends and peers and back to Jesus.

"Master, we have worked hard all night. My hands are cut and swollen from casting the nets out and drawing them back into the boat empty."

Simon saw a reassuring smile come across Jesus' face. "Simon, put out into the deep water and let down your nets for the largest catch of your lifetime."

Simon blinked, such words from a man who had never thrown a net in His life. He turned from Jesus. His eyes scanned his nets—years of backbreaking work were woven into each strand.

Everything was wrapped up in those nets—his income, his reputation, his security. It was crazy. No fish would be caught out there today. He had fished these waters all his life. He knew every inch of the shoreline, all the best fishing spots, and the depth of every cove. When he was young, he would dive from the bow of his father's boat and play happily with John and the others while his father and friends waited for the fish to begin their run.

No one knew the waters of Galilee like he did. There were very few things in life he knew and loved this well. And if there had been fish out there, he would have found them earlier this morning.

He turned back to Jesus intending to say no. But once his eyes met those of the Lord, he couldn't bring himself to do it.

Deep within the Teacher's eyes, he saw something that he had always longed to have within his own heart—a faith and a hope that seemed unshakable.

What difference could one fishing trip make? thought Simon. He smiled back at Jesus. "At Your bidding, Lord, I will let down the nets."

The order was given. Two of Simon's friends helped push the boat away from the shore while Jesus stood in the bow. The wind caught the sails and moved the vessel steadily out onto the cool, deep waters of Galilee.

Working the nets back over the side of the boat, Simon Peter couldn't help but notice the calm that had gathered. The lake had turned almost placid. Then suddenly the water stirred. From where Nicholas and the others were standing, it looked like rain dancing on top of the water, but it wasn't rain. It was fish. Hundreds of them.

Frantically, Simon Peter rushed from side to side tugging at the nets, but it was useless. The catch was too large, and the boat began to sink. He called to Andrew and John who had already cast their boats and were on their way to help. Simon Peter turned to Jesus and dropped to his knees. There was no way of knowing what the brawny fisherman was saying. All the people could do was watch from a distance in sheer amazement.

"It's a miracle!" the people shouted. "A miracle from God!"

Levi watched from the top of a hill and even before Nicholas was close enough to shout the news, he was aware that something much more than fishing was taking place on Galilee.

Who is this man? thought Levi as he listened to Nicholas's account. *How did He know where the fish were hiding? The people say He is just a carpenter. A common laborer turned teacher. Teacher?* The whole thing seemed ridiculous.

It wasn't long before Simon, riding a wave of well-wishers, appeared at Levi's table.

"How much?" Simon beamed. His smile was broad as he slapped a bag of money down on the table.

"How much?" echoed Levi.

"Yes, my taxes. How much will you rob me of this time, and for the last time?" added Simon.

"The last time?"

The crowd grew quiet as Simon looked down and then turned to where Jesus was standing across the street.

"I'm going to follow Jesus," he said, turning back to Levi. The smile returned to Simon Peter's face and his eyes grew wide with excitement.

"Simon," came Andrew's reassuring voice. "Jesus is waiting. Pay the man what you owe him, and let's leave."

Levi had known Simon all his life. Even though the two were bitter enemies, Levi respected Simon and to some extent envied his honesty and courage. Now as he studied the fisherman's eyes, he knew something had changed and it would never be the same. Strange as it seemed, Levi was saddened by Simon's words.

Levi reached for his Roman scale; the catch had been

weighed and sold. Now it was time to levy the tax. "You owe the fair amount. What was the sum of your catch?"

The crowd gasped. Another miracle? Levi never charged just the fair amount.

But this time was different; Levi did not pad his pocket by charging an extra tariff.

At first Simon Peter appeared stunned. Then a smile washed back over his face. "Levi," he said with a slight break in his voice, "we have found the Christ."

Levi's stare was cool as he tried to appear disinterested. "Pay your tax and leave. There are others behind you."

Simon Peter's eyes dropped. "I understand," he said and slowly opened his money pouch.

The tax was paid and Simon turned to go, but not without looking once more at the struggling tax collector. Levi sensed the hesitation and refused to look up. Instead, he pretended to be engrossed in counting the coins that lay before him.

Once Simon Peter entered the crowd, the celebration began. His was the largest single catch in Capernaum's history, three boatloads of fish. The streets filled with people who wanted to see Simon and the man who had sailed with him—Jesus Christ.

Levi looked down at his money box and then back up at the crowd. People were dancing, and many of the women were hurrying off to prepare the evening meal.

"Come join us, Levi!" shouted a passerby. Ignoring the call, Levi shuffled several parchment sheets together as he returned to the safety of his office. Deep inside, he longed for answers to the emptiness that surrounded him. Feelings he had not felt in years tore at his mind.

The celebration shifted and moved toward Simon Peter's house near the heart of the city. Levi was alone. Nicholas and Daniel had left for the day.

The day had gone quickly and the sun was now too heavy for the sky to hold. Its last refrain was a blazing good-bye across the Capernaum sky. Thinking things would seem clearer by the sea, Levi locked his office door and made his way down to the harbor.

There he was joined by an old friend, one of the few who had remained at his side since childhood.

"Levi, you look like a man with many problems. Tell me, what is so traumatic that it has stolen your joy?"

Levi was a little taken aback that Joash would notice. Apparently his mood was written all over his face. "Umm, I was thinking about Simon, and what happened today, and about this Jesus. Some say He is a messenger from God."

"You're not going to start believing that are you? Please, not you, Levi. He's just a teacher." Joash softly laughed. "And heaven knows we have plenty of those around here. So get a grip on yourself. Everyone has some type of wisdom they wish to impart. Believe me, the zealots would like to get hold of Him, and the Jews would like to ruin Him, and the Sadducees—who knows about those folks! But let me ask you, hasn't it been this way for as long as you can remember? One side wants this and the other side wants something else. And everyone wants the Messiah to come and save us from everything, especially the Roman government."

Joash drew closer, so close that Levi could feel the man's warm breath against his face. Looking directly into Levi's eyes, Joash smirked. "They even want to be saved from people like you, Levi."

Levi looked into Joash's steel-blue eyes. So, it was true. He was an enemy to his own people.

It was dark by the time Levi turned the latch on the gate to his home. Trying not to look worried, his wife, Rebecca, hurried across the courtyard. But her eyes told the story: she had been worried for quite some time.

"Levi, you're home! I was wondering. . .Well, it doesn't matter. You are home. That's all that matters. Have you eaten?"

Levi tried to smile as they walked arm in arm through the door to their home. "No, we were so busy today that I haven't had time to grab even a morsel of dried fish."

"Good, then we shall eat together. The children ate earlier, and I sent them off to bed." She realized that she was rambling rather than allowing her concern and frustration to show. "Josiah was impossible. I think he is at the stage in life where nothing pleases him, especially an admiring younger sister."

She had turned away from Levi so he would not see the tears building in her eyes. Softly she said, "I heard what happened today."

"And what did you hear?" he asked cautiously.

"I heard that you charged Simon the fair amount of tax."

Levi shrugged. "It seemed like the right thing to do at the moment."

"I also heard that Jesus of Nazareth was there and that Simon has become one of His followers!"

"Simon—Peter—or whatever he is being called, has left the fishing business. I don't know what this world is coming to. When a man like Simon hangs up his nets for a Jewish carpenter it has to be insanity. Therefore, I gave the man a break and didn't swindle the life out of him!"

"But, Levi, what you did was good, and God is pleased!"

"God?" Levi's mood changed instantly. "What does God have to do with a few taxes?" he snapped.

Her husband was hurting, and she could sense it. Now was not the time to pursue the issue. Levi was not ready to hear of God's love for mankind nor was he ready to hear that she too had made a decision earlier that day to follow the carpenter from Galilee. But something deep within her told her that a time was coming very soon when Levi would listen and believe.

"Never mind all that right now," she said, trying to comfort him. "You look exhausted, and I have dinner ready for you. We can talk about it in the morning."

Levi allowed the confrontation to pass, but inside his rigid will told him that all the mornings in the world could not change what he was feeling. Nothing could soothe his anger.

Trying to sleep that night was useless. Levi's thoughts were filled with anxiety and the look on Simon's face as he spoke about Jesus. Was Jesus really the Messiah? *If He is,* Levi thought, *He would never associate Himself with a tax collector.*

Levi rolled over and watched the glow of the lamp across

the room as the flame sent flickering shadows dancing across the wall. "If only I knew it was true," whispered Levi while wiping a tear from his cheek. "Maybe Rebecca is right. I'll think about all of this in the morning."

But the morning was already on its way for Levi. The small lamp across the bedroom shuddered as if blown by a slight draft and then went out.

It had been four days since Simon Peter's huge catch, and for the most part, life in Capernaum was getting back to normal. Livestock and imports from neighboring cities filled the streets as merchants hurried to buy and sell their commodities.

"Looks like the local trade is picking up again," said Levi as he entered his office.

Daniel lazily nodded yes to the enthusiasm.

"I must have been half crazy to let Simon off so easy. I could have made a bag full of money for myself and you, my friend Daniel. But as it ends up, I only helped Rome become richer."

Daniel shook his head in disbelief. "Let it go, Levi. There will be others just as successful as Simon. You'll gain your wealth from them."

"I suppose, but we much watch out for the man Jesus. If we are not careful, He may persuade the entire city."

"I thought you said He was nothing more than another Jewish teacher and nothing for us to be concerned about." Daniel's questioning was a little irritating. He knew the news on the street. Half of Capernaum was being swept away by the teachings of this young rabbi. Even the Jewish leaders were noting all that He did.

And He was back in the city today. Friends living next to Levi had tried to get him and his wife to go with them to a house where Jesus was staying. But Levi had refused and had forbidden Rebecca to go.

"People from everywhere come to hear Him speak," Levi said, "and there are new accounts of the miracles He has performed."

Daniel, who had been leaning back against the wall going over the tax assessment parchments, shook his head in disbelief. "I'm worried about you, Levi. You almost sound as if you like this man!"

"I admire Him—perhaps as one admires a fine chariot racer from a distance. It doesn't mean I plan to put money on Him. But yes, I admire the way He stands up to the temple priests. In their piety and long robes, they hold us in a bondage far worse than Rome, but no one does anything about it."

"Now I know you are crazy! The very name your mother gave you is connected with that place, and yet you are in constant opposition to its leaders. You were taught within the temple walls. What on earth has embittered your heart?"

Levi took a deep breath as if he were going to answer and then stopped. "It's not that simple. Let's just say we see things differently."

"Surely you don't see things the way Jesus sees them. I mean, He talks nonsense. Always talking about being poor in spirit along with being meek and gentle. It's crazy! He is telling the people that in doing this they will inherit a kingdom!"

"There is wisdom in that, Daniel. The temple rulers think they are the ones whom God will lift to His holy place, but see that poor beggar over there?"

Levi pointed to a broken shadow of an old woman moving up the street.

"I knew her when I was young. She has been looking for Messiah to come all these years, barely a denarius to her name. Yet, she goes to the temple and prays and gives whatever she has. Would God refuse her entrance into His kingdom? I tell you, it's people like me and the priest that will have to answer to Him."

"I didn't know you felt that way," Daniel's voice dropped off. "All the years I have worked for you, I thought you were only interested in tax gains but never in people like that old woman."

"There was a time . . ." Levi paused and the silence grew between them. Suddenly Levi straightened as if to push the emotion of the moment away. "But . . . what am I paying you for? To stand here and listen to my murmuring? I want you to go over to the market and check on several merchants there. Daris has conveniently forgotten my address, and he owes us plenty."

"I'm sorry if I . . ."

"If you what?"

"Pressed you into talking more than you wanted to."

"You are a true friend, Daniel." Levi sounded tired but sincere. "Now get going or I'll forget to pay you this evening."

The crowds pressed against Daniel as he moved out into the street. "The Teacher is coming!" someone shouted. "Make way, the Teacher is coming!"

It must be Jesus, thought Daniel. *I wonder if Levi will see Him pass?*

As Daniel turned to cross the street, Jesus stepped out in front of him. Simon Peter was beside Him along with Andrew and James. The crowd opened just enough for Jesus and His disciples to move through. Some called His name, others shouted words of greeting.

Stopping close to Levi's tax booth, Jesus turned to Simon Peter and asked, "Peter, do you know the man who operates this business?"

"All of Capernaum knows him. His name is Levi, and he does Rome's dirty work. We all pay for his sins."

"Tell me, do you love him like a brother?"

"Love . . . Levi, Lord? Like a brother?" Peter's voice stopped.

"Wait for Me here; I'll return shortly." Jesus touched Peter's shoulder in affirmation as He walked away.

Levi had just finished a transaction and was engrossed in his thoughts. It had been an exceptional day financially. He planned to celebrate his own miracle tonight with food, dancing, and wine—yes, Roman wine!

Suddenly a hush surrounded him, and looking up, he saw Jesus standing before him.

As their eyes met he heard Jesus say his name. "Levi."

Jesus stretched out His arm and touched the tax collector's shoulder. "I want you to come and follow Me."

An immediate warmth flooded Levi's heart. But Satan's arsenal was ready to unload a rapid succession of questions on Levi's mind. Was he hearing Jesus correctly? Was Jesus calling him to be a part of His band of disciples? Surely not. Didn't Jesus know who he was? He was a Jew, yet he stole from his own brothers. He was the lowest form of Jewish citizen. Certainly Jesus knew this. Perhaps he was going to single him out to chasten him or ridicule him. That was an unbearable thought—not here, not in front of all these people!

Then Christ's words, "Follow Me," fell back over his mind. *How can I follow Him?* Levi concluded. *I'm a sinner.*

Levi's lips parted with the intent of saying no to Jesus. He knew he did not deserve such grace, such forgiveness. But then he could not let this moment pass. It might be the only chance he would ever have to get things right between him and God. Did this mean he believed that Jesus was from God?

Jesus reached out and grasped Levi's arm as the crowd stared in disbelief. Slowly the tax collector stepped forward. Then, unexpectedly, his outer garment caught the corner of the money box sitting on the table and sent it spinning to the ground.

The second step would be much harder knowing that all the money was now lying on the ground beside them.

What do you really want, Levi? a taunting voice chimed inside of him, *the money or life with Jesus?*

Jesus was waiting for Levi to respond. He knew Satan's pull was strong, but God's pull was stronger still.

"Follow You, Lord?" Levi's eyes glistened with tears of joy. "Yes, I will follow You."

Jesus smiled and drew the former tax collector into His embrace. "From now on, I will call you Matthew—gift of God." He placed His arm around Matthew's shoulders as they walked away from the tax booth.

Meanwhile the disciples waited near the edge of the street. They had seen Jesus embrace the man that for so long had taken advantage of them.

And though no one spoke, each wondered what would happen when Jesus returned to them.

From several paces away, Jesus called to the group, "Peter, Andrew, James, John—this is Matthew. From now on, he is to be like a brother to you."

Shame and the thought of his sin had lowered Matthew's head. For a moment no one moved, then one of the group's members stepped forward.

"I'm Peter, Matthew."

Matthew lifted his head and looked into the eyes of the former fisherman. They were full of love and acceptance.

"I'm Matthew, Peter." And with those words the two men embraced.

A WINDOW TO GOD'S HEART

If Matthew were alive today, we might think he had it all—a good business, a loving wife, family, and home. On the surface his life looked great, but deep down inside there was a tidal wave of emotional unrest brewing. Lack of acceptance, even hatred, characterized Matthew's life, and the fact that he was Jewish only inflamed the situation.

Where could someone like Matthew go to find true fellowship? Not to the Romans; they detested Jews. Nor could he go to his childhood friends; he was a tax collector, and these were the very people he taxed heavily each day. More than likely, Matthew's friendship consisted of people much like himself—society's outcasts. People who were spiritually depraved and in their depravity lead others astray. Often they were lonely, angry, and forgotten individuals. The very thing they hated the most about their lives was all they knew how to do. These are the people Jesus came to save.

No sin is greater than God's forgiveness. Only His love is capable of removing sin's stain from our lives. He is the God of second chances. And regardless of your past, present, or future, Jesus loves you and accepts you unconditionally.

Luke and Mark tell us that Matthew left everything to follow the Savior. He gave no thought to what others would think of him. Nor did he try to retrieve his tax collection box. The Savior touched an eternal part of Matthew's soul, and all that mattered was his obedience. Obedience is the mark of true discipleship, and Matthew had that mark.

Only Jesus could see into the depth of Matthew's heart. Only He understood that hidden in the darkness of Matthew's life was a deep longing to know and be known by God. What Jesus did for Matthew no one else could do. He offered Matthew unconditional love and acceptance. In fact He even called him a gift of God. This is what Matthew's name means in the Greek.

Obedience is the first step to becoming a disciple of Christ.

The next step is acceptance: your acceptance of Christ and His forgiveness of your sins. Many people think their sin is too deep for Jesus to forgive, but this is not true. God in His grace promises to forgive every sin.

Once your sins are forgiven they are erased for eternity. Jesus never drags up past sin in an attempt to condemn and ridicule. Only Satan seeks to accuse those who belong to God. Take a moment and think back over your life. Have you truly trusted Christ as your Savior and Lord? If not, you can pray to receive Him right now. Tell Him that you are sorry for all that you have done and that you want to turn from a life of sin and death. Then ask Him to come into your life and save you.

Once you have done this, you are a new creation in Christ. He is now alive within you, and nothing can change the fact of your salvation. Pray that God will give you a deep desire to know Him better and to serve Him forever.

CHAPTER 3

Window of Healing—*The Faith to Believe*

"Out of my way, woman! Some nerve you have showing your face on the city streets!"

"Be gone," shouted another voice. "Go back to your own home and away from us!"

"You're unclean, and we want no part of you!"

Frightened and weeping, the shadowy figure covered her face while burying her eyes in the soiled, tattered cloth that covered her head and shoulders. Tears streamed down her face, a face that still had the light of youth on it though years of physical distress had left it etched with pain.

Her momentum had been cruelly stopped, and for a moment she felt as if all breath would leave her body. There was no peace, no rest, and no hope for her. She had tried everything imaginable and still found no relief to her suffering.

The shock of rejection never grew old. No matter how many times she was faced with its stark reality, the hurt was always fresh and new. Thoughts of hurrying home to hide flooded her mind, but what would be gained in leaving? She needed water, and if she did not fill her jar now, she would be forced to return later in the afternoon. By then the streets would certainly be filled to capacity.

Years of suffering had stolen her hope as well as her joy, a joy that was once so contagious people came from all parts of the city to see her. But now she was alone and forced to live outside the city gate with others, who like her, were considered spiritually unclean.

In the beginning, she maintained her faith and believed that somehow God would provide the right physician to cure her. Yet her search had yielded nothing more than an empty purse. In paying physician's fees, she used all the money her husband was able to save before his death. Widowed and without a way to make a living, she was at the mercy of the temple priest.

"Why? Oh, why must this be my burden to carry alone?" she cried. "It is too heavy! All that I have is gone. Oh, God, surely You can save me, or is it that Your arm has grown too short to answer my call?"

Without realizing it, she had stepped out into the center of the street and raised her clenched fist toward heaven. Suddenly, the thrashing of a passing cart jarred her back into reality.

"Move, old woman!" shouted the driver as he laid a stiff strap across his oxen's back. The cart was practically on top of her. She quickly jumped out of its way, leaving her water jar behind to be crushed by the turning wheels. Without a backward glance, the driver rumbled down the street and out of view.

Silently, she bent down to touch what was left of the jar.

"Just like my life," she said, fingering the pieces. "Shattered. Fragmented. Broken and wasted. Of what value am I to anyone? I am even too poor to die."

Tears filled her eyes. The fight was finally over. This was the final blow. She could take no more humiliation. In turning to go, she heard the voices of a large crowd somewhere in the distance. Thinking it was no more than another celebration, she readjusted the covering over her head and shoulders and began to make her way home.

The streets were deserted except for a young lad scurrying along in front of her.

"Son!" she called out. "Please, son!" The boy turned in her direction. "I won't hurt you. Can you tell me where everyone has gone?"

His boyish face was full of life and laughter. "Haven't you heard? Jesus is teaching near the seashore!"

"Jesus?"

"Yes. Jesus of Nazareth. Where have you been? Everyone has heard of Jesus! My father says that He may even be the One whom the prophets said would come to save us."

She had heard of this Man. Many believed He was a man sent from God. His teachings were like none she had heard before, but then she had known only stolen moments of His messages, when in the crowd's excitement, she was able to blend in to the background unnoticed. Yet to say this Man could save Israel, or for that matter anyone, seemed ludicrous.

"Save us?" She laughed. "Save who? Certainly not me! No one can save me, not even God Himself."

The lad winced at her words and looked as if he wanted to run. She had spoken irrationally and realized it.

"I'm sorry. It's just that I have been sick for so many years. Perhaps the sickness in some way has affected my heart. I know I am bitter, but I have prayed for so very long. I have asked God to heal my suffering, but He has answered my cries with only silence." Her voice broke as she began to weep.

"Today of all days, why would you want to cry? Haven't you heard? Jesus heals those who come to Him. I overheard two of the men who are traveling with Him talking, and I know where He will be passing. If you want me to, I will take you there."

She paused and nearly broke into laughter. He had not heard a word she had said. "Even if I agreed to go with you, I could never get near enough to tell Him of my disease. He is a Jew, and the people would not allow it."

"It doesn't matter. Jesus is not like that. He has friends all over the city. I have seen Him heal people. Once He even healed a man who was born blind. Could anything be harder than that? I know He will help you, if you will trust Him. I'm going to tell Him about my baby lamb. His mother left him when his foot got caught in the rocks above the city. The leg was broken, and now he's lame."

Studying the lad's face and listening to his words, the woman couldn't help but sense the hope and faith that he had in Jesus. "Does He really heal people?"

"Yes! And it doesn't matter who you are or how old you are."

The lad didn't wait for an answer. He simply grabbed her

hand and off they went through the city, tumbling along his youthful shortcuts and scampering up the hillside that overlooked the Sea of Galilee. There they stopped so she could gather her breath.

A short distance away, she could see throngs of people waving and shouting to a common looking man standing on a large rock.

"What is He doing?"

"He has been teaching them about God and how they can live their lives for Him," the boy said, smiling as he moved ahead. "But we must hurry. There will be plenty of time for you to hear about this later."

Suddenly the woman's expression changed as doubt filled her heart. *Why should I continue this search?* she thought. *It's ridiculous. I could never get close enough to talk to this Man, let alone close enough for Him to treat my illness.*

"Why have you stopped?" the lad called.

"If only you knew my story. I have searched for years to find a cure and there's none. Please, you hurry on along, or you'll miss Him. I'm too old and too tired to try any longer."

For a moment the youth balanced back and forth—torn between what to do. Should he leave her? What would happen to her?

"I don't know why you are hurting," he said. "But if only you will believe, I know Jesus can help you."

Reaching out, he touched her hand. "I know this Man is from God, and He may know how to help you or at least know someone who can. Won't you at least try?"

Looking up through tears of doubt, she suddenly felt a tingle in her heart, something motivating her to take his hand.

The boy smiled and said, "I'm Simeon."

"Well, Simeon, my name is Rachel. I guess we had better get going or we will miss Jesus."

This time he held her hand even tighter as they went down the hillside and across the rocky areas near the shore. By the time they had reached the bottom, the crowd had shifted and was now moving rapidly toward them.

Simeon's voice was anxious as he shouted for her to stay close beside him. But caught up in the emotion of the moment, she strayed and was soon swallowed up in the crowd of onlookers.

Then for a reason known only to God, the crowd parted in time for her to witness the strangest sight. An official from the synagogue was kneeling at the feet of Jesus. He wept as Jesus listened and then knelt beside him. The moment was intense and seemed urgent.

The woman could not hear their words, but rarely had she seen such compassion radiating from anyone's face. She suddenly knew that if she could get close enough to touch Jesus, her life would be changed forever.

But the crowd was pressing hard against her. Suddenly her view of the two men was blocked. Now everyone was moving toward her again. *Oh, where is Simeon?* she thought. Then, pressed by the crowd, she fell, slamming her face hard into the ground.

Dirt filled her mouth, and panic pulled at her heart. She was dazed and frightened. Yet from deep within her a voice called out, "Lift up your eyes, and reach out your hand. Your redemption is drawing near."

Jesus was close, so close that she could sense His presence. She stretched out her hand and touched His hem.

Then . . . there was peace. Glorious peace washing over her. Cleansing every corner of her being. Immediately the demons of sickness and isolation that had haunted her for years were hurled to the farthest corner of time's existence. The sickness and disease that had tormented her minutes before crumbled in the presence of God's Son, and the warmth of His acceptance ministered to her emotions. With one touch the darkness was banished, and she collapsed back onto the dust of the earth.

The miraculous had happened. The flow of blood had stopped, and the pain and cramping had ceased. She was healed, and there in the shadow of love's wings all of heaven celebrated the victory.

By now Jesus had stopped and turned in her direction and with a voice that thundered through her soul asked, "Who touched Me?" Then turning to His disciples He said, "I tell you someone touched Me, for power has gone out of Me."

One of the men nearest Jesus seemed frustrated. "Lord, how can we possibly know who touched You? The people are all over us."

But knowing all things, Jesus left them and approached the woman lying on the ground behind Him.

His voice softened. "Daughter, why did you touch Me?"

Tears of joy covered Rachel's face as the memory of the

years of pain and suffering flowed out of her. Nothing was left unsaid to her Savior.

"Daughter," He said, His voice marked with love and compassion, "your faith has healed you." Peace and security rested within His eyes. "Yours is the kind of faith that springs from God. He has restored you. Go now; you're forever free from your suffering!"

The bondage that had held her captive for years was broken. Jesus had healed her just as Simeon had said He would. But her healing went beyond the physical; it had touched her entire life.

"Lord," she whispered as she looked up at Jesus.

Suddenly a voice broke in, "Jairus! Why bother the Teacher any longer? Your daughter has died!"

Jesus rose and turned to the man whom Rachel had seen with Him earlier. "Do not be afraid, Jairus. Believe in Me, and your daughter will be returned to you."

"Peter, John," called Jesus, "we must go to this man's daughter."

Turning back for a final look in Rachel's direction, Jesus found she had been joined by several other women, and together they praised God for the miracle He had performed.

"I am free!" shouted Rachel. "Gloriously free and clean. Jesus has healed me, and I must tell everyone what He has done!"

David, a young merchant, ran to her side. His face was filled with emotion. "Did the man named Jesus heal you?"

"Yes!" shouted Rachel. "He has given me new life!"

"Then I will give you whatever you need for the temple sacrifice."

"Two turtledoves and two pigeons," replied Rachel without hesitation.

"They're yours. I'll see to that. And in eight days when you offer your sacrifice to the temple priest, the angels of God will cry out in joy over you."

"I have a feeling they already are," she called out to him as he headed back into the crowd.

"They already are!" she shouted again while raising her hands in praise to heaven.

It had been three weeks since she had seen Simeon. On the day of her healing, he had vanished into the throngs of people. Suddenly, looking out from the courtyard of her daughter's home, she noticed a small but capable figure making his way down the street. Even from a distance, she knew it was Simeon. But what on earth was he carrying? A few feet closer and she knew. It was his lamb.

"Simeon!" called Rachel.

Simeon's face brightened. "Rachel! I haven't seen you since that day . . . I mean, I lost you in the crowd, but I saw you talking to Jesus and heard the people rejoice in your healing."

"It was just as you said, Simeon. Jesus healed me, but even more so, He healed my bitterness and gave me a new life."

Placing the lamb gently in front of her, Simeon continued to stroke its head. "I knew Jesus would know exactly what to do."

"Oh, Simeon, your lamb. Did Jesus heal your lamb?"

Simeon's chest rose in pride. "Oh, yes. See, he's as good as new. You would never know that his leg was once broken."

"But how did you catch up with Him? He left so quickly."

"I waited for Him. My father has always told me that if I wait in prayer for what I need, God will answer. This time He sent Jesus my way. When I told Him about my lamb's leg, He said He understood and not to worry, the lamb would walk again." Simeon paused and took a deep breath. "That very evening as I was changing the animals' straw in the stable, I noticed my lamb standing beside the door. He had walked across the room just like Jesus said he would."

"What a precious joy, Simeon! You must love your lamb very much."

"I do, but now my father says he must go back to the fold. He has tried several times to follow me when I leave the house to go into the city. He needs a shepherd, someone to watch over him so he won't stray," said Simeon bravely.

Rachel could feel the hurt within his voice.

"But guess what . . ."

"Tell me," said Rachel, bending down to pet the baaing lamb in front of her.

"My father has promised to teach me all there is to know about herding sheep. One day, I will sleep out under the stars with my lambs. I will protect them and love them and nothing will ever cause me to leave them."

Rachel's eyes sparkled at the thought.

"Jesus is like that," said Simeon.

"Like what?" asked Rachel.

"A shepherd! He told us the other day that He was the good Shepherd. He said, 'A shepherd is always willing to lay down his life for his sheep.' I would lay my life down for my lamb."

Rachel's eyes flushed with tears at the analogy. She, too, remembered the words of Jesus as He taught them about the things that were to come. But it wasn't just the words of Christ that had stirred her heart, it also was the love and devotion He showed to all who came to Him.

Watching Simeon continue his journey brought a smile to her heart. Especially as he allowed the lamb to follow at his side.

"My dear Simeon," whispered Rachel. "Jesus is our example, and I know that He loves you and me and everyone so very much. Even your little lamb is dear to His heart. And you are right, my son. Jesus has promised never to leave us."

A WINDOW TO GOD'S HEART

According to Jewish Law, Jesus should never have stopped to converse with this woman. But He did and in doing so risked becoming unclean at her touch. Through His act of compassion for this woman, we learn something very intimate about our Savior's love. First, God's love toward us is unconditional, and second, He is always in tune with our specific needs.

Jesus is aware of your deepest needs and wants to bring a solution to each one perfectly and completely within His timing. For many people this may mean immediate results. For others it may mean a season of waiting. But regardless of the time frame, Jesus is always available to strengthen and encourage you (Isa. 43:18–19; Ps. 68:19).

More than likely, this woman had never met the Savior. Perhaps she had seen Him in the city and even witnessed the miracles He performed, but she had never talked with Him. Everything that could be done for her had been tried in an effort to bring healing. In her search for a cure she had exhausted her financial resources and probably those of her family as well.

Hopelessness and discouragement met her at every turn. In the morning when she woke up, her condition remained unchanged. In the evening when she blew out the candle, her body continued to wrench with pain. For twelve years she had suffered. There was nothing left of the life she once had. All the spontaneous joy and laughter were gone. She was consumed with one thought, one dream, one goal—to be made well, to be healed, to know the comfort of peace and rest in the warmth of her family's love. Only Jesus could change her life, and reaching out through the darkness of her disease she dared to touch the hem of His robe.

Nothing is strong enough to separate us from the love of Christ. No sickness, no disease, no sin—nothing. No matter who you are, what you have done, Jesus will come to you if you will call out to Him. He was not repulsed by this woman's condition, nor is He repulsed by our sin. Instead He is moved with compassion any time one of us calls out to Him. His words to this woman were words of grace and good news: "Daughter, your faith has healed you."

God has a goal in mind for suffering.

His purpose in allowing this woman's sickness to continue was to bring her to the end of herself and then to salvation through faith in His Son. So many of us want to take charge of the situation the moment we sense things going awry. But God wants us to learn to bring everything to Him; nothing is too small, nothing is too large. Ask Him to show you what His goal is for you in the trials you are facing.

Tell Him that you want His best for your life.

Many times God chooses to heal or deliver us from tragic situations. However, other times He doesn't. This is when we need to know God has not forgotten us and is working to bring good out of such tragedy. Romans 8:28 promises us that God is working all things together for our good.

Make sure your life is submitted to His plan.

He knows the future He has for you, and He knows what it will take to accomplish His plan in your life. Pain, sorrow, joy, love, laughter, and much more are all needed to help us to grow into the likeness of His Son. His ultimate goal for your life is that you reflect the image of Jesus Christ to others.

Whenever you face adversity of any kind, remember that you are not alone. Jesus is our burden bearer. And in faith you, too, can reach out to touch the hem of His robe. Ask God to give you wisdom and courage to face the circumstances of your life. Make a commitment to wait for His answer no matter how long it takes. God always honors obedience, and if you will honor Him with your love and life, He will never lead you astray.

CHAPTER 4

Window of Love—*Benjamin's Story*

Even though it was late spring, the night air was still quite cool. The day's rain had brought a sweetness to the air, and Benjamin could sense it as he hurried through the city streets. In his heart, he wanted to run to be near his friends, but he refused to yield to his emotions. Nothing, not even a faster pace, must draw attention to his journey tonight.

Suddenly there were footsteps behind him. Pulling his cloak up around his neck and head, he dropped back into the shadows of a nearby building. His heart raced as the strangers approached. Then from somewhere within his mind a voice calmed his fears: *Peace, My peace I give to you, not as the world gives. So don't let your heart be troubled and do not be afraid. I am near.*

There in the darkness as the soldiers passed in uneventful conversation, Benjamin smiled to himself. He was safe and Jesus was at his side. Slowly he exhaled and whispered. "Thank You, Lord, for protecting me."

As he watched the two figures disappear around the corner of the next building, his hand slid over the leather pouch attached to his side to check its security. "And please, Lord, protect my steps as I continue."

Jesus Christ had been recently proclaimed Messiah in the synagogue by the Christians of Rome—an action not favorably received by the government nor by the Jewish leaders. Claudius, the Roman emperor, had immediately ordered all of the Jews out of the city. That was earlier in the week. Benjamin had arrived in Rome without any knowledge of the emperor's proclamation.

The news was both bitter and sweet, victorious and discouraging. The fact that Christ was recognized as the Messiah was an emotional boost to believers living in and outside Rome. On the other hand, because of Claudius's sudden rage, many Christians would face persecution. Already believers were forced underground to worship. The meeting Benjamin was to attend this evening had been rescheduled and moved from the home of his dearest friend, John, to a catacomb near the outlying areas of the city.

Benjamin had promised John that he would meet with the growing group of believers as soon as he had completed his visit to Jerusalem. He felt certain it was time to return to Rome. In fact, he carried words of encouragement from the church in Jerusalem. Words that the faithful needed to hear, especially now that so many were being forced to leave the city.

Drawing in a deep breath, he thought, *Where will they go? Surely not to Jerusalem. The political unrest there is even more intense.*

Up ahead he could see the entrance to the underground

chamber. Placing his hand on the top of the stone archway, he bent over to listen for any sign of movement. It was dark, damp, and very silent.

Lord, I know You will show me the way. Help me find my friends so they may hear Your words of encouragement to them. I can't see in this darkness, so, please, guide my steps with the light of Your love. With those thoughts he stepped inside the stone tunnel and began his journey through the darkness.

After several moments, his eyes adjusted to his surroundings and he could see a warm glow at the end of the corridor. Usually the tunnels were lit with torches throughout, but today's earlier wind and rain must have blown out the ones nearer the entrance.

As he moved toward the light, the tunnel turned slightly to the left. Benjamin felt the sudden impact of the hard, cold stone surface against the side of his face. *Easy, Benjamin, looks like you need to bear to the left here.*

With the light growing brighter, Benjamin was sure he would find his friends. He could already feel their arms of love hugging him. But as he stepped into the chamber, he realized no one was there. *They must be meeting in another part of the catacomb, but where?*

Just beyond the single torch he noticed the chamber emptied into another tunnel where he saw at least two more torches.

I wonder . . . perhaps they are in there, but farther down the tunnel. If so, I'll be the last one to enter by this torch. He reached up and pulled the torch down from its wall brace.

No sooner had he passed the next chamber than the tunnel divided once again. An updraft blew hard against him, and the flame threatened to go out. The frustrations of his journey to Rome seemed to be gaining ground. And standing in the windswept catacomb, he could feel discouragement building.

He drew a deep breath and leaned back against the stone wall. Its rough texture provided a natural seat. It had been three months since his last visit to the city. John was with him when they had discovered this place. Did he dare confess that he was lost?

Benjamin shook his head in disbelief as he fought feelings of weariness and loneliness. *I know You are here with me, Lord. But I remember a time when I didn't know if You would ever be with me again.* Tears filled his eyes at the memory.

I also remember the first day I saw You. We have traveled so far since then. Yet there are so many more miles to travel, so many more people to tell of Your love and grace. He leaned his head back as his thoughts carried him back to a small hillside outside Jerusalem and his childhood.

"Jesus is coming! Hurry! The Master is coming." Benjamin heard the shouts and stepped out from behind the rocks that overlooked the Sea of Galilee just in time to see the man they called Jesus walking away from a small fishing boat.

From behind him he heard yet another voice, "Benjamin! Mother said for you to share your lunch with me." He turned back to his sister and frowned as he tightened his arms around his lunch—a small basket of barley rolls and two tiny sun-dried fish.

I'm a growing boy, thought Benjamin. *How will I ever be*

*as strong as Father if I continually have to share food with
my sister?*

"Did you hear me, Benjamin? Benjamin!" shouted Ruth as
she glared at her younger brother.

He wanted to stick out his tongue at her, but he didn't.
He held himself back. He was almost thirteen and that
meant he was almost a young man. If he was going to be
grown-up, he had to start acting grown-up. Just one more
month and no one would ever call him a lad again, he hoped.

"A barley loaf and half of a fish—that's all," said
Benjamin, matching her glare.

"I don't know how you think I will survive on that. I'm
hungry, and there are so many people. How could I buy food,
even if there were a merchant nearby, especially now that your
childish curiosity over some teacher from Nazareth has separated us from Uncle Josiah?"

Each year their uncle took his brother's children with him
to Jerusalem to celebrate the Passover feast. They always left
early so Benjamin and Uncle Josiah could spend extra time in
the temple praying. Benjamin's parents would follow later
after securing the family's business. His father was a tanner,
and in Benjamin's eyes, he was one of the best.

Late in the evening at bedtime he would tell Benjamin
stories of Abraham and Isaac. Benjamin's eyes would grow
wide with excitement as he listened to the heroics of God's
servants. Then just before nodding off to sleep, he would ask
his father to tell him once again about the man who would
come one day to save Israel from Roman persecution, the One
who would be called the Messiah.

"You are going to get me skinned," his father always said. "You know your mother wants a well-rested young lad at her side in the morning, and if I continue to stay here, she will skin us both!" The two would laugh as his father gave into his pleas.

"Father, I heard you talking with Nathum this morning about the rabbi, the One of whom Uncle Josiah has spoken. Is he the One who will be called Messiah?"

The warmth of a father's smile and the reassurance of his hug were gifts Benjamin knew well. Bending down he gathered young Benjamin into his arms. "My son, you ask the strangest questions for a lad your age."

"Well, Uncle Josiah says . . ."

"I know, I know what your uncle says." His father paused in thought. "I pray He is, Benjamin, but no one knows for sure. And if He is—"

"I know, I know," Benjamin said, echoing his father's words. "He will want a well-rested young lad at His side one day."

"Yes, and so will your mother in the morning. So sleep well, my son."

How could this man be a Messiah? thought Benjamin as he watched Jesus and His followers climb the hillside. He didn't look like a Messiah, only like an ordinary man.

Benjamin looked at the scene. Everything seemed so fresh and so new. The clouds were crystal white and fluffy as if they had been marvelously painted on a backdrop of soft blue sky. Wildflowers dotted the rocky areas of the freshly cut hillside.

Jesus sat down at one end of the field and immediately was

joined by a small group of children. He embraced their laughter with His own. The sight pulled at Benjamin's heart, and he, too, longed to join their fun. Yet, he remained at a distance, hands tightly gathered around his lunch and eyes filled with wonder at the sight of Jesus.

Two of the men at Jesus' side were counting the people. *They will never be able to count that high,* thought Benjamin. By now the field was packed with people who had stopped to rest while journeying to Jerusalem.

As Jesus stood to speak, Benjamin moved closer so he could hear as well as see the face of the man whom his uncle believed was the Messiah. But Jesus seemed troubled and stopped talking and gazed at the multitudes surrounding Him.

Benjamin had seen that look before in his father's eyes. It was after the birth of his baby sister when the family had very little to eat. Business had been bad, and he had heard his father crying. So far as Benjamin knew, his father had never cried before that time.

"Son." A voice interrupted Benjamin's thoughts, and looking up he saw the face of a man who moments before had been at Jesus' side. Benjamin swallowed hard. His first thoughts were of Uncle Josiah. *Had something happened to him*?

"My name is Andrew. What's your name?"

"Benjamin," he replied cautiously.

"Well, Benjamin, there are many people here and no food for them to eat. Would you be willing to let the Master bless your lunch and share it with those who are hungry?"

Benjamin looked down at his basket and then over at Jesus. It was all he had to eat, but from deep within he sensed an inner urging calling him to release his hold on the basket. Looking up at Andrew, he nodded yes before he knew what he was doing.

"Great! Then I will take you and your lunch to the Master."

As the two approached the disciples and Jesus, Benjamin overheard one man discussing wages and the amount of money it would take to feed a crowd this size. Finally another man spoke up and said, "Lord, just send the people away."

But Jesus paid no attention to their comments. He had turned His attention to Benjamin and the small lunch basket.

"Lord," began Andrew, "there is a lad here who has five barley loaves and two fish. Perhaps this food will help, though I know it is very little among so many."

Smiling, Jesus turned to His disciples and said, "Have the people sit down."

The disciples sprang into action and began motioning for everyone to be seated. Some of the onlookers complained, while others laughed at the idea of being fed a small boy's lunch.

Jesus stood beside Benjamin and picked up the basket. He lifted it up toward heaven and prayed for God to bless and multiply it, then turned and placed the fish in one basket and the loaves in another.

Before his eyes, Benjamin saw the fish multiply. Where there were two fish now there were four, then six, then on and on until the baskets filled and overflowed. In amazement Andrew spun around and looked at Jesus. Their eyes locked in urgent embrace as he fell at the Master's feet.

"Lord! There is so much!"

"Yes, Andrew, there is always an abundance with God. And for those who trust in Him there will never be a need that goes unanswered. Now help your brothers feed My flock, and when all have eaten, gather the leftover pieces, so that nothing will be lost."

Benjamin looked up at Jesus with wide-eyed, childlike laughter. "You made my lunch grow!"

"My Father in heaven did, Benjamin. You gave all that you had unselfishly, and He is well pleased with you."

"God is pleased with me?"

Jesus drew him close and caressed his head. "Yes, son. He is pleased every time we give Him something we hold dear. That lunch was all you had, but you were willing to share it with those who had none. This is what He desires, that you would give from your heart, and you have done just that. Great is your reward in heaven, because you have trusted the One whom He has sent."

Then Jesus stood up and began to teach the people concerning God's provisions. And as they ate the bread and the fish, He explained how the Father would provide for all their needs if only they would believe in the One the Father had sent.

After all had eaten, the disciples gathered the leftovers and placed them before Jesus. There was enough to fill twelve baskets.

Seeing the miracle, the people shouted with joy, and several men stood and proclaimed, "This is the man the prophets spoke of, the One who would come into the world. He will be our king!"

Jesus turned to His disciples. They looked shocked. Was

the kingdom of God standing before them, and were they so blind that they had not even seen it coming?

"Jesus!" Judas said as he reached toward the Master, but the Lord turned quickly to Peter. "We must go from here."

"But, Lord, where will we go? They want to make You king."

"Take the others and go back to Bethsaida. I will join you later. I must be alone with My Father."

Jesus then turned and walked through the crowd. He passed unnoticed by those celebrating His coming kingship. Out over the grassy knoll and through the wildflowers He walked. His hands drifted slightly above the flowers as they swayed up to meet His touch. He continued alone though not completely. Benjamin had seen Him leave and was following close behind.

Jesus would not go into the city for the Passover. Instead He was going to a quiet place on the nearby mountainside. Benjamin's heart raced. *If He makes it to the crest before I shout to Him, then He will be gone, and I will never see Him again.*

However, Jesus knew He was being followed and decided to allow the distance to grow slightly between them and the crowd below. Once they were over the rise in the hillside, He turned to the lad who was tenaciously climbing the slope.

"Benjamin, why are you not back with the others?"

"I want to come with You—like Andrew. I want to follow You. I will be thirteen next month and no longer a lad!"

The moment was irresistible and Jesus couldn't let it pass without acknowledging the spirit and faith of His new friend.

"Did you follow Me because you saw the miracle or because you believed?"

"No one could do what You did today unless He is from God. My Uncle Josiah believes You are the One who will come to save all of us." Benjamin stopped and took a deep breath. "So, I guess I believe."

"Then you must believe and follow Me in your heart—loving the Lord your God with all of yourself. Where I am going right now and what I must do you cannot know. But I tell you the truth, we will meet again."

Standing a few paces away from Jesus, Benjamin broke into a full run and the Savior caught him and lifted him up into His arms. *So what if I am almost thirteen?* thought Benjamin. *It's OK to be hugged just once more before I become a young man.* With that, he buried his face in Jesus' shoulder.

The next time he saw Jesus was in the winter of A.D. 30. He had stood for hours with his friend John in the cold to see the Master once again. In the spring, Benjamin's father had almost died. No one knew how to treat the disease that was causing his suffering.

Benjamin had taken on many of the responsibilities of his father's business. He was older, but no matter how much life changed, he still thought of Jesus every day, His words and His message to the people.

If only I could tell Him that even though some resent Him, I believe in Him with all my heart, thought Benjamin.

"Some are saying the Teacher is outside the city," said John. "But Mother is expecting me to be home early. So I can't go with you this time. I hope you find Him and can tell Him about your father."

"I will. Thanks," said Benjamin. John was like a brother to him. And as the two parted, Benjamin delivered a playful, strong arm to his friend's shoulder. He had told John all about Jesus and John had believed. The two had dreamed of becoming Jesus' disciples, but family problems in both their families held them back.

The only reason Benjamin was in Jerusalem today was because of business and his uncle's willingness to travel with him. John's family had moved to Jerusalem only two months before. Benjamin missed their friendship. But at least he had someone to visit whenever he was in the city.

Jesus was coming up from Bethany, where He had been teaching. Time after time, the Pharisees had tried disrupting the crowd that followed Jesus with their accusations.

Benjamin had longed for this day—the day when he would see Jesus again. But the people were pushing and pressing on him from every side. Getting close enough to speak to Jesus seemed impossible.

Many thought Jesus would go into the city, but He didn't. Instead He left the area and headed north to the safety of the hillside. As the crowd followed, Benjamin hurried to keep up. Finally their journey ended with three of the disciples turning the people back.

The crowd began to disperse until all had gone except Benjamin, who sat down on the side of the road and fought back tears while trying to gather his thoughts. Picking up a rock, he tossed it as hard as he could across the roadway and into the field in front of him. Then he broke down and wept. He had planned to tell Jesus about his father. No one knew just how sick he really was, not even John.

How would he ever find Jesus again? He needed to return home, and Uncle Josiah was probably waiting for him. Tears welled up in his eyes as he caught a glimpse of the edging around his cloak. It was worn and frayed. The family was out of money, and the weight of all the earnings now fell on his shoulders. It was too much for him to bear alone.

Jesus, if only You were here, I would tell You. I am still following You in my heart even though I can't follow You physically right now.

"Then the heavenly Father is well pleased with you, Benjamin, and so am I."

Benjamin opened his eyes to see Jesus standing over him along with Peter and Andrew. "I thought You were . . ."

"Gone? A shepherd never leaves his flock. I know My sheep by name, and yours is dear to Me," said Jesus as He reached out to touch the youth's shoulder. "However for now, I must continue My journey. Peter and Andrew will see you safely back to the city gate."

Then Jesus' eyes deepened and the familiar smile turned serious. "I want you to know something, something you will need to remember one day very soon. No matter what happens, I will never leave you or forsake you. That's a promise, and it's forever."

"Then I will follow You forever," said Benjamin with his chin held high and shoulders pulled back.

For a moment Jesus studied the sight. To Him, Benjamin

looked like a soldier, freshly commissioned and ready for battle. A wave of joy passed over the Master's face as He turned to Peter and John. "Such as these belong to the kingdom of God."

Benjamin's faith did not go unnoticed, and the disciples nodded yes.

"Come on, Benjamin, we had better get you back to the city, before it gets too late," said Peter.

"Oh, and Benjamin—" said Jesus as they turned to go. "Your father is waiting for you. When you get home there will be much rejoicing."

Benjamin's heart leaped at the sound of the words. He could hardly wait to tell his father all about Jesus.

It was dusk by the time they arrived at the city gate. Benjamin could tell by his uncle's steps that he was worried. When he looked up to see Benjamin with Peter and Andrew, his worried look eased.

"He's been with the Master," said Andrew. "And we wanted to make sure he made it back to you safely."

The old man smiled. "So, Benjamin, you have found the Messiah?" said Uncle Josiah.

"Yes, and I don't care what others say. I want to be one of His disciples."

"Sounds as though you already are, my son," replied his uncle.

Both watched as Peter and Andrew disappeared in the darkness. They were headed back to Jesus and to some distant campfire where God's message of love for all mankind would be taught, and in Benjamin's heart, he, too, traveled with them.

Over the next few months, journeymen brought news of Jesus to Benjamin's hometown. Each week he and his father talked through the Law of Moses and the prophecies of the prophets. They believed Jesus was the One the prophet Isaiah had written would come.

"I'm grateful for you, Father," said Benjamin one morning shortly after his return from Jerusalem. "I knew in my heart that you were well even as I traveled home. Coming home only made it more real."

"Jesus?" asked his father.

"Yes, I don't understand how He knew, but as I walked away that day He told me that there would be much rejoicing when I arrived home."

"And there was, my son. God is so good to us. He and He alone healed me. And Jesus is His messenger to us and to Israel. But I'm afraid the people have chosen to believe otherwise. They can't leave their tradition, and they can't accept Him as a prophet. Many say He is a blasphemer," his father said, looking away and shaking his head. "There is trouble waiting for Him in Jerusalem, Benjamin. The Pharisees will see to it."

His father's words hurt, but they were true. The course that God had charted seemed all too firm. The Passover was coming, and Benjamin's family planned to make their usual pilgrimage to Jerusalem. Perhaps Jesus would come into the city this year and take part in the celebration. If so, Benjamin wanted to find Him and warn Him of the growing evil.

Jerusalem was not a place of peace, and John's words tore at Benjamin's mind.

"You are lying to me!" shouted Benjamin. "John, tell me you are lying. How could they convict an innocent man?"

John stood shaking with tears streaking down his face. It was the hardest thing he had ever done, telling his best friend that Jesus had been arrested as an enemy of Rome and was at that very moment being taken to a place outside the city to be crucified.

"John, tell me you're lying. I'll forgive you." Benjamin shook his friend wildly in an effort to change what his ears had just heard. "It can't be true. It just can't. Why Jesus? Don't they know He is the Messiah? I must go there. I must see Him before . . ." Benjamin's legs weakened under him. The shock was more than he could bear, and he sank to the ground.

"How can they convict a man for something He never did? I mean, every day He was among the people, teaching in the temple. Why now? Why Jesus?"

"No one knows why. Perhaps the Jewish leaders were threatened by His words. Nevertheless, the people don't understand. They've been caught up by the emotion of the moment. Pilate tried to save Him by offering to release one prisoner as a token gift for the Passover, but the people wanted Barabbas—a thief and common criminal—released instead of Jesus."

"He should never have come into the city, John. He didn't last year. Why this year? Why Jesus? Why? You must take me to Him."

"Benjamin, you won't even recognize Him. As I waited for

your arrival near the Damascus Gate, I saw them lead Him out to Golgotha. Much of the skin on His face and upper body was torn away. They flogged Him, Benjamin."

"It doesn't matter. He is my friend, and my Lord. I must go. I told Him I would follow Him forever. If that includes following Him to a Roman cross, I will do it."

The distant rumble of thunder signaled an approaching storm. As the two young men pushed their way through the crowded, narrow streets and outside the gates of the city, lightning cracked across the sky and many of the onlookers left to find shelter. With a howling wind pushing against them, Benjamin and John approached Golgotha.

Three crosses formed dark, silhouetted images against the Jerusalem sky. So it was true. Jesus was going to die. All the hopes and dreams, all the times Benjamin had planned to join Jesus' followers, seemed lost forever.

"That's far enough!" shouted the Roman guard as he anchored his spear across Benjamin's path.

Glaring into the soldier's eyes, Benjamin pushed past the extended arm and continued a few feet more until he was at the foot of the cross. His eyes lifted and beheld the sight of his dying Lord.

As Jesus raised His bloodied head in an agonizing effort to breathe, something welled up from deep within Benjamin. This would be the last time he would see Jesus, his last chance to tell Him of his love and allegiance—the last time he would see Him alive.

"I will follow You forever, Jesus. Forever!" His voice was

unchallenged by the sorrow and pain surrounding him. Instead it rang out with purity and determination.

And where the blood drifted down from a crown of thorns, he saw the Savior's eyes and knew that his voice had been heard.

By now the wind was whipping at his clothes. A cruel rain beat against him and the others near the cross. The thunder rolled and pounded against the earth, and the lightning threatened to tear the sky in half.

Somewhere between the flashes of lightning, Benjamin lost consciousness and fell facedown at the foot of the cross. Awakening moments later, he tried to open his eyes but they were filled with mud. He rubbed frantically at his face to wipe away the dirt and debris but it was useless.

He held his face up to the sky so that the rain could wash his face and prayed. "God, Jehovah, I'm so afraid. I know I want to believe in Jesus. Please help me to understand. Why did He have to die?"

He had never felt such silence surrounding him. It was as if he were conscious that someone was near. *John,* he thought. *Where is John?* But John had moved back to find shelter. Only Benjamin and a small detail of frightened guards remained at the cross. And they had backed away in fear of God's wrath.

Then Benjamin noticed something moving toward him. Trailing across the hillside it moved with speed and agility along the rocks and over the rain-drenched ground. Painting a path toward him, the light seemed to sear the ground as it passed. It stopped behind the cross that bore the Son of God and then dissolved into it. Emerging from the front, it engulfed

Benjamin and drove him backward while forcing his face upward to the cross.

His mind was filled with the memory of the last time he saw Jesus outside of Bethany, and he recalled the Savior's words.

"A shepherd never leaves his flock. I know My sheep by name and yours is dear to Me. But I want you to know something very special, something you will need to remember one day soon. No matter what happens, I will never leave you or forsake you. Never. That's My promise to you and to everyone who believes in Me."

At first the memory hurt. Then Benjamin wondered. *Could it be? Is Jesus still with me? But how?*

Standing, he whispered, "Forever, Jesus. I will follow You forever." Instead of hopelessness, there was peace. Instead of fear, there was a sureness that somehow, someway, Jesus was still with him.

It had been twenty years since he stood at the foot of the cross. Since that time, the Jewish leaders had continued to dig their own graves. And despite followers being persecuted to the point of death, Jesus' popularity had grown. Not even Rome in all its power and splendor could put an end to God's ministry through His Son.

Three days after Christ's burial, reports surfaced that He was alive. The women who were with Him at the cross in death were the first to see Him alive at the burial site. Later that same day, He appeared to His disciples.

Benjamin had even been a part of the crowd who witnessed the Father taking His Son and our Lord up into heaven.

So Jesus' last words were not those spoken on the cross. No. Instead, His last words were spoken in victory through His resurrection. They were words of hope and a future. Words that spoke of His return one day, and until that day His followers were to be witnesses of His life and message throughout Jerusalem, Judea, and the world.

"Well, are you just going to sit here all night?" The familiar voice brought a smile to Benjamin's face. John had found him and was moving toward him through the darkened catacomb.

"You found me. Thank God, you found me."

"I told the others that you were probably lost. Let me see, was it the first turn in the tunnel or the second that fooled you?"

"The first."

"Well, at least you stayed put and didn't continue on and end up under Caesar's palace."

"The palace! No! Thankfully."

"Benjamin, what were you thinking about? I mean, you didn't even flinch as I approached."

"Jesus . . . and His care over us."

"I thought so. Was it the promise He gave you that captivated your heart?"

"Yes, but it's not just my promise, John, it belongs to all of us. He promised never to leave any of us. That is why we can have hope even in this darkness."

"You are right. And it is the reason we can sing of His love and hope. In fact I want you to hear something. Come on, the others are waiting."

John stopped just before they reached the opening to the chamber where members of the early church of Rome were gathered.

Gently, a soft and worshipful melody filtered through the catacomb. There in the darkness surrounded by the defeat of death, the song of eternal life was sung.

And leaning toward Benjamin, John whispered, "It's worth it, Benjamin. Every moment of this life is worth living for Him."

Benjamin nodded and smiled an affirming yes as he reached out and grasped his friend's shoulder.

"I have word from our brothers in Jerusalem, especially from James, the Lord's brother." He opened the leather pouch as he stepped inside the torchlit chamber.

This was why the Savior had come and died. That all men and women might come to know Him as the Son of God. It was not an easy way to live life, but it was the only way to know life eternal.

Opening the parchment, Benjamin began to read: "James, a bondservant of God and of the Lord Jesus Christ, to the twelve tribes which are scattered abroad, Greetings.

"My brethren, count it all joy when you fall into various trials, knowing that the testing of your faith produces patience. But let patience have its perfect work, that you may be perfect and complete, lacking nothing.

"If any of you lacks wisdom, let him ask of God, who gives

to all liberally and without reproach, and it will be given to him. . . ."

A WINDOW TO GOD'S HEART

Paul the apostle writes to the Corinthians, "Though I speak with the tongues of men and of angels, but have not love, I have become sounding brass or a clanging cymbal" (1 Cor. 13:1). Love is the reason Jesus came to earth—His love for you and me. No matter what your life holds, God loves you.

Nothing is strong enough to shut out His love, and nothing can stop Him from loving you. Nothing you've done or will do in the future can cause God to love you less. He knows that when you do fail, the one thing that will keep you and bring you back to His side is the love and forgiveness that flow from Calvary's cross.

But God's love is not cheap. It cost Him everything, the death of His Son and the separation He felt when Jesus died for us. We often forget that God has emotions. That He, too, has feelings though they are perfectly in tune with His sovereign nature. When Jesus was on earth, He cried, laughed, experienced anger, joy, and love. He loved us so much that He freely gave Himself for us.

How can you come to know the love of God better? A good beginning is in prayer. You can ask God to make you aware of His personal love and devotion for you.

Love requires a commitment.

God made the greatest commitment that has ever been made when He sent His Son to earth to die for our sins. His mission was to provide a way to eternal life. Jesus did that when He took our place at Calvary.

You may be in a relationship that you feel is requiring too much of you. Before you walk away, ask God for His wisdom in your situation. Pray for Him to help you love your friend or family member with the same love He extended to each of us at Calvary. Relationships are hard work. God is taking a lifetime to prepare you to live with Him in eternity.

George Matheson once wrote, "If I would know the love of my friend, I must see what it can do in the winter."† When things get rough, we often find ourselves looking for a way out of a relationship. Instead of hanging tough, we leave and hang out someplace else. At any point, Jesus could have thrown His hands up and declared us ignorant beyond belief, but He didn't. He had stick-to-itiveness and was and is completely committed to us.

Love is not self-seeking.

God's love for you and me is not self-seeking. He had one goal in mind in coming to earth, to provide a way for us to live throughout eternity with Him. Everything God did from the Garden of Eden to Calvary was motivated by love. Discipline, guidance, protection, instruction, fellowship, and more have all come from the overflow of God's love. King David wrote, "I love you, O LORD, my strength. / The LORD is my rock, my fortress and my deliverer; / my God is my rock, in whom I take refuge. / He is my shield and the horn of my salvation, my stronghold. / I call to the LORD, who is worthy of praise, / and I am saved from my enemies" (Ps. 18:1–3 NIV).

71

All we will ever need is already taken care of in Jesus. He is your Provider, your Strength, and your Encourager. If you fall, He is the first one to reach out to lift you up. The woman at the well had had seven husbands. Shame so engulfed her life that she could not even go to the well to draw water at the same time of day as the other women. But Jesus took time out of His schedule to meet her and to offer her His love, forgiveness, and hope. In Him she found acceptance and the living water that every one of us thirsts for. What is your most intimate need? You can take it to the Savior without any shame and tell Him all you are feeling because His love for you is the greatest love of all.

Love keeps no record of past wrongs.

God keeps no record of our past sins and failures. Once He forgives you, you are forgiven. There's no need to try to work for God's approval. He accepts you unconditionally and will be beside you to teach and guide you throughout life. Sealed for eternity, we bear His bloodstained mark as witness of His forgiveness and life within us.

Love never fails.

Jesus told His disciples He would never leave them. They probably thought He had left them with His death, but they were wrong. John was the only one that stayed by the foot of the cross. The others were in hiding, their faith weakened and their hopes dashed. When it appeared that all was lost and confusion besieged their minds, Christ stepped into the room.

Whatever you face in life, Jesus will face it with you. His

love never fails. You can call out to Him anytime, anywhere. He is always near. The story of Benjamin is fictional. But the love and commitment he had for Jesus is very real. Many of those who followed Christ died because of their faith. Others traveled to the ends of the earth carrying the gospel message. In both cases, love had captured their hearts, and no matter what happened, they had met the Savior and nothing would be the same again.

† Mrs. Charles E. Cowman, *Streams in the Desert* (Grand Rapids, MI: Zondervan, 1980), 263.

CHAPTER 5

Window of Forgiveness—
Love's Eternal Message

Matthan looked across the small cell at his friend Joram. Joram had been bleeding badly, but now the bleeding had stopped and he was sleeping.

Matthan's own right hand had been crushed by the Roman guards during his arrest. With his body wrenching in pain and his mind refusing to rest, Matthan listened to the noises just beyond the wall of his cell.

There were the usual murmurings of prisoners. He had grown accustomed to hearing those over the years. The sarcasm of the guards only made him feel sick for having been caught. But the noise from the city street had a much different effect on him. Filtering in through the cries and the curses, it reminded him of the uneasy state of his situation. The noise represented a point of reference that balanced between freedom and captivity, life and possible death. Both Matthan and Joram were soon to face Pilate's council for sentencing.

Matthan hoped that would never happen. Two years ago, his life was caught up in petty thievery. Then he met Joram, and together they tapped into the more affluent Roman society with their crime.

Feeling very much alone, Matthan realized he had no one to blame for his condition except himself. When he was young, his mother had begged him to change his lifestyle. She was a woman who was dedicated to God. His father did not really care whether God existed or not. Matthan had grown up adopting his father's religious perspective. Even if there was a God, he saw no need in believing in Him. What difference did it make if one person worshiped God and the other worshiped the things of the world?

His father was a merchant and had taught Matthan at an early age to admire the things money could buy. "The important things in life belong to the man who has silver and gold in his pocket," his father would say with a wink of an eye.

In the end, Matthan rebelled against both parents and began to steal the things he wanted. Yet in all his thievery, he never could satisfy his inner hunger for love and contentment. The man he called "Papa" stayed on the road for long periods of time, traveling great distances. When there was extra time for the family, he often spent it with market girls instead of Matthan and his mother.

Resentment grew between him and his father. Finally, the two squared off after Matthan had been caught stealing from a local market. He could not remember why he took the merchandise; perhaps he acted on a dare from friends. Or perhaps he reasoned it was better to gain some type of attention from his father than none at all. Whatever the reason, it seemed insignificant compared to his father's anger and rage.

"Never again!" shouted Zacharius while pointing at his son. "Never again will a son of mine steal and remain under my roof!"

Matthan countered the attack with even harsher words. Years of neglect and pent-up emotions emerged as he yelled back, "Why, so you won't look bad in the eyes of your friends?"

Social position meant everything to a merchant. It affected the type of merchandise he sold, where he lived, and even how his family dressed.

His father's face changed from rage to instant hurt at his son's words. Never before this day had Matthan raised his voice to his father. Now the two were attacking one another freely. The older man broke down and wept.

"Son, I always wanted something much better for you than the way I was raised. You were to have the best!"

"What was wrong with the way you were raised, Papa?" asked Matthan. He remembered his grandparents well and, though they were poor, they were happy. He often recalled the songs his grandfather taught him as a lad. They were Jewish songs. Some celebrated life, others were songs of God's forgiveness and restoration.

"There was never enough to eat or enough clothes to wear." His father's voice shook with emotion. "In the winter we nearly froze from lack of heavy outer garments."

There was passion in the older man's voice, and for the first time Matthan realized how he longed for his father to hold him and tell him he loved him. Risking rejection, he drew near to his father, but it was too late.

"And you, you would take all that I have provided and toss it away on a moment of petty thievery. If you are determined to live the life of a thief, then so be it. Out of my house!"

Matthan stood before the older man in shock. He couldn't believe what he was hearing. His mother, crying softly in the next room, had also heard her husband's sentence.

"Now get going, or I'll throw you out myself!" shouted Zacharius.

Those were the last words he heard his father speak. No time to say good-bye to his mother, no time to gather a small bedroll. Just enough time to turn and gaze one last time on Papa. From that day, rebellion ruled Matthan's heart.

"I don't even know where you are, Papa," Matthan whispered, incensed at his thoughts.

Joram stirred, and Matthan realized he had been thinking out loud.

"You are talking to yourself again, my friend. Who is this phantom that you chase in your thoughts?" Joram's question was a valid one. After all, they had been friends for some time, and Matthan had never told him the truth concerning his father.

"My father," answered Matthan.

"Your father? Well, is this man even alive that he should consume your thoughts?"

"I don't know. Perhaps that's why I think so much about him. Maybe I would like to know that myself," said Matthan, half smiling and turning away.

"No, Matthan. Your thoughts and dreams are not of longing, but of hate."

Matthan fought an instant desire to fight. A small bug scampered across the hard, packed dirt floor in front of him. With one swift blow Matthan ended its life. Then he glared at Joram, his eyes filled with tears. "I don't know where he is."

The silence between the two men was broken by approaching footsteps. Matthan rose and looked through the awkward opening in the door.

"They are coming for us," he said anxiously.

"Relax," said Joram. "We have slipped through the system before, and we will do it again."

"I don't think so, Joram. The man we attacked, the one with the small gold nugget ring, was a Roman official. You saw the insignia. I heard one of the guards say that he had died. So we're as good as dead men."

The soldiers were at the door and, for the first time, Matthan saw a stiff wave of concern come across Joram's face.

"On your feet!" shouted Sergius, commander of the prison guard. "This will be the last full night of sleep either one of you receive. The next one will be spent in the company of the gods!" Leaning forward to within inches of Matthan's face, he sneered. "And may they deal ever so severely with you. Today, however, it is Pilate's turn."

Sergius reached out and grabbed Matthan by the shoulder of his cloak.

Joram struggled with one of the guards, broke free, and raced through the door. There was a sickening thud outside the cell, then Joram staggered back through the door followed by two Roman guards. Matthan cried out at the sight. Joram clutched desperately at a sword protruding from his chest.

With eyes bulging, Joram crumbled to the floor in a twisted knot of frozen fear.

Suddenly there were hands under Matthan's arms, lifting him through the door and dragging him down the darkened corridor. He struggled to look back, hoping against hope that his eyes had been mistaken, but all he could see was Joram's lifeless hand lying in the doorway.

Matthan was not the first prisoner to stand before Pilate today. The line was long. Two guards remained at his side as they waited for Pilate's entry into the praetorium.

"Why did you refuse to listen to Satius the last time you were judged by Rome?" A familiar voice jolted Matthan from his thoughts of Joram and what had happened moments before.

His eyes, now heavy with fear, looked up to see the face of Demetrius, a Roman guard who had shown a mild interest in him the last time he was imprisoned in Jerusalem. At that time, he had urged Matthan to clean up his life and get rid of Joram, but it was not something Matthan wanted to hear. Each time Matthan appeared before a Roman court, his sentence became stiffer and more painful.

Just two months before, Cornelius, an official of Rome, had warned him that death awaited him should he appear before another Roman council. He had ordered Matthan beaten and released. Rome could live with petty thievery. It was viewed more as a nuisance than a violent crime.

But the moment Matthan stepped up his actions to include Roman citizens, he had cast lots on his life. This time he was not the winner. The state dealt heavily with murderers. Often the beatings accompanying the sentence were so severe that crucifixion became a welcome escape from the pain.

"There is no escaping this time, Matthan," said Demetrius as he leaned forward, but Matthan looked away. "The day you drew your sword to the neck of a Roman official was the day you signed your own certificate of death."

Tired of his words, the soldiers rebuked Demetrius and motioned for him to move on. The call came that Pilate was waiting for the prisoner. As the guards shoved him through the doorway, Matthan tripped and fell upon the cold stone floor of Pilate's courtroom. Helpless, he lay at Pilate's feet.

"Such a pitiful sight," came the scoff. "Are you even aware of the charges against you?" Pilate's eyes were intense.

Never in his wildest imagination did Matthan think he would have to face Pontius Pilate.

"Do you realize the man you killed on that obscure highway was a state official, a friend of Herod's family, and proconsulate of a Roman province?" Pilate's voice boomed through the chamber. He stopped for a moment and studied the man lying before him. "Obviously you don't know."

Pilate drew a deep breath and turned to the window that looked out over the countryside. From there he could see beyond the walls of Jerusalem. "This place has become a scourge to me," he said as he took several swift steps back toward Matthan. "But I intend to rid it of infectious diseases like you. Recorder, read the sentence, and remove this man from my sight."

Pilate's cloak swirled and snapped into position as he

turned to go. Matthan never had a chance to speak in his own defense.

"The prisoner is found guilty of murder against Rome," the recorder said. "He is, therefore, sentenced to death by crucifixion no earlier than sunrise and no later than noon tomorrow."

Later that evening Matthan slowly opened his eyes and tried to focus on his surroundings. Every part of his body ached from the beatings he had received that afternoon. They were but preludes to his crucifixion. He wasn't sure how or even why he was still alive. The blows had shattered several of his ribs. Now, lying facedown on the floor next to a small pool of vomit and blood, he could feel his lungs struggling for air.

It seemes late in the evening, but how late? Is it dawn? Have I been unconscious all night? Frantic thoughts of his impending execution filled his mind. Suddenly, he was aware of footsteps outside his cell window. *Perhaps*, he thought, *it is a group of guards coming to get me!*

However, the footsteps he heard seemed strained and muffled, as if to hide something. There were whispers. *Guards never whisper,* thought Matthan. *They shout their commands and expect immediate results.* No, whoever was outside his window did not want to draw attention.

Studying his physical condition, Matthan thought, *If I can just make it to the window, then I can pull myself up to see outside.* With the number of voices increasing, Matthan's heart raced. Slowly he slid across the floor of the cell. Painfully, he rose to his knees then lifted his hand high enough to grasp the bars of the window and with great care raised himself up.

Through the steel grayness of the night, he could see a group of men approaching the guard station. Another group, consisting of Jewish leaders from the temple, awaited their arrival. Roman guards led the way as the men passed through the gate.

A slight sigh of relief passed over Matthan. They were definitely not coming for him. Instead, it looked as if they were escorting another prisoner to the praetorium.

Their exchange was brief before entering the building. But even in the moonlight, Matthan recognized their prisoner. He was a young Jewish rabbi named Jesus. All of Jerusalem was up in arms over His teachings. Some believed God had sent Him to the Jews. Others thought He was simply a good man with reasonable things to say. But Matthan had heard enough on the streets to know that the Jewish leaders hated Him and wanted Him dead.

A centurion opened the gate to the courtyard. The procession entered and disappeared in darkness, leaving two lonely looking men waiting outside the gate.

Matthan's legs gave in to the pressure of his weight, and he slid to the floor. Dawn and death were ever before him. Fear began to rise within him. There in the silence of the night, he cried out; but there was no one to hear, not his mother or his father, not even God. He was alone, and thoughts of the approaching morning tore at his mind. He knew what crucified men looked like. He had seen their bodies hanging for days on crosses outside the city.

Food for vultures, he thought. "Oh, dear God, help me!" screamed Matthan. "If You are really there, please help me." His cries softened as Matthan waited for an answer, but there was none, only the darkness and a hopeless repose.

The swift opening of his cell door startled him and sent him pushing back against the wall. He must have passed out again sometime before dawn. Two guards lunged for him, and with whips flaring, they struck him across his right shoulder.

"Save it for the procession," snapped Sergius as he held back the arm of a young centurion. "If you kill him here, then you'll carry his cross to Golgotha!"

Sergius turned to two guards waiting in the rear near the door. "Barabbas is to be freed. Release him and escort him out of the city. If I see him back here again, I'll be tempted to kill him myself."

The guards moaned. Barabbas was a notorious murderer. There wasn't a guard alive who didn't want to see him dead. He was also a zealot whose life was committed to pressing his political viewpoints on the Roman government.

Turning his attention back to Matthan, Sergius kicked at the prisoner's feet.

"Get up!" His tone turned bitter. "You're a fortunate devil, Matthan. Today, you will be crucified next to a madman who thinks He's a king, only He has no kingdom."

Laughter broke out among the guards as Sergius continued, "And if that's not enough, He claims to be the Son of God. So just think, He may very well make you an heir to His throne."

Again the guards laughed as they pushed Matthan around the cell in gamelike fashion.

"Let's go," said Sergius, motioning for the guards to take Matthan out into the courtyard.

The sunlight was blinding, and with one strong push from his attending guard, Matthan found himself lying facedown in the dirt. A Roman centurion raised his foot and placed it on the back of his head and shoved his face into the ground.

Another prisoner waiting nearby and strapped to a huge wooden crossbeam screamed for mercy, but the guards were consumed with laughter and threw cups full of vinegar and water in his face.

"Two thieves and a madman for today's crucifixion—not bad for a day's work," hissed the commander.

As the wooden crossbeam came crashing down across Matthan's back, the weight of his crime ripped at his soul and fear ravaged his emotions.

"Get up!" yelled the centurion standing over him. His whip found its mark again as every nerve ending in Matthan's body came to life.

With his body tightened and braced to lift the enormous weight, Matthan tried to stand but instead broke under the strain and fell to the ground.

The guards immediately sensed a kill and jumped him like dogs on a wounded prey. At best, he would be dragged to Golgotha.

Lying at the base of the wooden stake that would soon form his cross, Matthan could hear the other prisoner cursing the guards. Only half aware of his surroundings, he prayed seriously for the first time in his life. He prayed he would see his mother's face, know his father's embrace, and find forgiveness in their eyes. However, this was not a moment for answered prayer; the last prisoner was approaching, and the atmosphere grew even more tense.

Sergius paced the length of Golgotha with long, striding steps. He was worried that the crowd following the third prisoner would be large and volatile. One wrong word or action and he and his men could easily be facing chaos.

These temple rulers with all their whining will be the end of us all, he thought. *I can't believe that Rome has stooped to their bidding once again. Doesn't Pilate know how the people follow this Jesus?*

Sergius could see the procession approaching in the distance and urged his men to hurry. Three soldiers held Matthan, while a fourth centurion looked up at his commander anxiously.

"This is not the easiest job," he mumbled while raising the oversized mallet. Fear swept over Matthan's face as he imagined the spike being driven into his wrist. His eyes widened from the shock of its impact as wrenching pain filled his mind and overflowed into cries of agony.

"Why am I not dead?" screamed Matthan. Then he fainted.

When he regained consciousness, his cross had been lifted into place, and he could hear the cries and curses of the crowd surrounding the crosses. He struggled frantically to free himself, but the spikes tore at his flesh. He was trapped, and there was no way out of this agony.

He fought to breathe, but the weight of his body hanging on the cross was suffocating him. The searing pain from his impaled feet left him limp and helpless. Finally, he raised himself high enough to allow air to sweep down into his lungs. From his pinnacle, he could see the crowd below. Some wept softly while others shouted curses at the man to Matthan's right.

"So, You were going to destroy the temple and build it back in three days— save Yourself!" shouted a man dressed in the clothing of a temple priest.

"If You are the Son of God, come down from the cross!" called another voice. It was then that Matthan remembered seeing Jesus outside his cell the night before. The man on the cross next to him was Jesus!

Matthan's throat ached as he longed to call out to Him. *Any dry whisper would never be heard over this crowd,* he thought, as the people continued their verbal assault.

"Are You the Christ? The king of Israel?" Laughter followed. Then another man shouted, "Come down, and then we will believe that You are who You claim to be."

"No," shouted yet another man. "He trusts in God; let God deliver Him! Or maybe Elijah will come and save Him." After each round of insults, more laughter followed.

Through all of this Jesus remained silent until at last He cried out toward heaven, "Father, forgive them. They don't know what they're doing." Then His head dropped.

Matthan directed his attention to a woman near the base of Jesus' cross. A young man was with her, and together they wept and clung to one another.

The sight touched the very core of Matthan's emotions. *Was that Jesus' mother?* How Matthan had hungered all his life to know the compassion he witnessed between those three people. But there was no one there for him, not even today, his last day alive.

In his loneliness he found himself wanting to reach out to Jesus though he didn't fully understand why. Perhaps, he wanted to hear someone say, "You're forgiven." Something! Anything! But to die like this with no one to say I love you was the loneliest kind of death.

Before Matthan could speak, the man on the third cross joined the crowd's cursing. "If You are the Son of God, save Yourself and us!"

Without realizing what he was doing, Matthan countered the attack. "No!" he shouted. "This man has done nothing wrong. Don't you fear God now that you are dying? We deserve to die for the evil we have done, but this man has done nothing wrong. He is innocent!"

Matthan turned to look at the Son of God. There, deep within the eyes of Christ, was the love and concern he longed to know. Suddenly nothing mattered but speaking to Jesus.

"Jesus . . . ," gasped Matthan. "Will You remember me when You come into Your kingdom?" Their eyes met, and a sudden flood of emotion from deep within Matthan's soul came spilling out.

"Today, My friend," said Jesus, "you will be with Me in Paradise."

God's love was instantaneous, and despite the pain and

death, Matthan could feel love's pure and unconditional embrace. The anger and fear that had controlled his life faded.

Matthan struggled to speak, but the fluids collecting in his throat and lungs began to choke him. He was going to die, but he was not alone. Jesus was with him.

A cold, hard rain began to fall as the earth shook without compassion. The people who had gathered for the crucifixion fled for cover.

Jesus cried out,"*Tetelestai* . . . It is finished!" and collapsed.

A short time later the wind and rain stopped and a guard stepped up to the base of Matthan's cross. He took a moment to make a mental note as to where his club should strike the prisoner's legs. The Jews wanted the men removed from the crosses due to the approaching Sabbath. Broken legs would insure quick suffocation and certain death before sunset.

Through half-opened eyes, Matthan watched as the guard raised his club and took aim. The man's full weight accompanied the swing and a searing pain shot through Matthan's body. Uncontrollable nausea swept over him as he hung in the balance between life and death.

But suddenly the darkness of death was broken as a series of flashing white lights shattered his thoughts. Matthan was aware of the guards surrounding the crosses, but now their voices were fading. A strong force of light came close to him. Its power was impassable. It paused, then moved away and waited at a distance. Matthan's mind shuddered as if it wanted to stop and render his spirit. Matthan was fighting to stay alive.

Another streak of light approached. This time it pierced his mind, and the pain subsided. Continuous flashes of light rolled over him, and, with each one, the pain eased a little more. But the darkness maintained its rage for control of Matthan's soul. Without warning, it reached out and engulfed him.

From the back of his mind Matthan sensed a gentle wind beginning to blow. It swirled past him, calming his emotions. Another stronger light broke through the darkness. He could feel it drawing him closer to a misty brilliance.

Taking in a deep breath, Matthan experienced the filling of God's perfect love. It beckoned him to let go of the control he had left on his life. "Release your hold," called the light. Then suddenly it was gone again.

Matthan envisioned himself holding tightly to a long rod that represented his human control over his life. He knew if he let go he would lose control, yet he also realized he was dying.

The light returned and spoke once again to his spirit, "Let go and the Lord God will give you rest."

Finally Matthan relinquished his control and began tumbling through an all-besieging darkness. "I'm falling!" he screamed as his mind grabbed out at eternity. "I'm falling, Jesus. Help me!"

Suddenly Matthan stood in the fullness of the light. "Matthan." His spirit heard the voice of God.

"Matthan." The voice broke through his fear, and Matthan's spirit turned to respond.

"Matthan." A warmth broke through the cold and flooded his mind as Matthan's spirit yielded its control to the Savior.

Lifting his hands ever so lightly, Matthan stared at the

places where huge nails had been. There was no blood, no sign of struggle or pain, and no sorrow. But how?

"Matthan, it is I. And I love you."

The darkness was gone, and love had come at last to Matthan's heart. A warm and inviting light covered him, and small flashes of light darted around him. They drew close and enveloped his mind with words of praise and glory to God.

"Holy, Holy, Holy is the Lord God Almighty!"

"Holy, Holy, Holy is the Lord our God!"

"All of creation is full of His wondrous glory and praise!"

"How great and powerful is the Lord God Almighty!"

Eyes that moments before were bound in darkness now fully viewed their Savior and Lord, and Matthan fell to his knees in worship. It was Jesus! . . . Life everlasting! The promise of God!

A WINDOW TO GOD'S HEART

Our world is starving for acceptance, forgiveness, and love. Yet with one sentence, "Today you will be with Me in Paradise" (Luke 23:43), Jesus offered all three to a man who had been condemned to eternal torment. So stark is the contrast that it's hard for us to grasp the mental picture the Scripture portrays. In intense agony and with His last earthly breath, Christ saved a common criminal, someone society had cast aside and wanted dead. But even on the cross, Jesus had one goal in mind and that was to offer God's eternal forgiveness, hope, and salvation to those bound up in sin.

Many people try to clean up their lives before coming to Jesus. They think if they work hard enough they will get their lives in acceptable order, but they can't, not without the Son of God. Salvation is a free gift from God. It's not something we can earn.

Nothing you can do will make you more worthy than you are right now. When God saved you, He saw Christ's death on Calvary's cross as sufficient payment for your sins. The freedom you enjoy as His child was paid for in full by His Son's death.

Jesus will never hesitate to meet you right where you are, regardless of the sin or the immoral entrapment. The thief on the cross had two choices: he could call out to Christ or he could side with those who were mocking the Lord. He chose to call out, and he received eternal life.

God has a plan for your life. Only you can do what He has called you to do (Jer. 29:11). Even before He saved you, He knew all there was to know about you, and He loves you. Nothing can erase His love.

When temptation comes and you yield to its allurement, instead of condemning yourself, go to Jesus in prayer. Tell Him all you have done and all you are thinking. Acknowledge your sin and receive His forgiveness, then get on with life.

The Christian walk is a lifelong journey. God never meant for it to be lived out in a week, month, or year. Along the way your faith increases as you learn to trust Him. And the more you know about Jesus, the more you will love Him. And the more you love Him, the more you will want to please Him and be like Him.

In the end, His love will draw you completely unto Him, and you will notice that old sins and habits have disappeared and that you have become a brilliant reflection of His love and joy.

CHAPTER 6

Window of Commitment—*Forevermore*

"You are a chosen generation, a royal priesthood, a holy nation, His own special people, that you may proclaim the praises of Him who called you out of darkness into His marvelous light." (1 Peter 2:9)

Once they were among Jerusalem's elite Jewish leaders. Now, broken in spirit, they were like sheep without a shepherd, lost in a nightmare of despair. With their long priestly robes blowing in the wind, the two men watched as the crosses were raised into place—a call to death that was reserved for the most hardened criminals. Yet neither Joseph nor his friend, Nicodemus, understood why the life of a young Jewish teacher had to end here.

Nicodemus drew a deep breath, as he studied Joseph's tearstained face. "How could this have happened?" he asked. "I should have done more to prevent this." His voice tightened with guilt.

"But Nicodemus, you tried. They would not listen to you, nor would they listen to me. All they could see was how this one man challenged their beliefs and traditions. Little do they realize that with His death their world will change even more." Joseph's eyes questioned what they were now seeing—a Roman soldier struggling to hammer a wooden plaque above the head of Jesus.

"The inscription reads, 'Jesus the Nazarene, The King of the Jews,'" said Joseph. "Pilate ordered it written in Greek, Latin, and Hebrew so that everyone could read it. You can imagine, Caiaphas was furious!"

"You're right, Joseph," said Nicodemus. "Nothing will ever be the same. This man's life has changed us, and we must bear the shame of His death."

Nicodemus and Joseph, both members of the Sanhedrin, had been friends for years. When they were younger they debated the Torah and memorized the writings of the prophets together. Joseph, always the insightful one, believed the coming of the kingdom of God was near. Nicodemus believed but was more cautious in his belief. There had been so many years of silence without Israel hearing anything from God concerning the coming Messiah. Yet Nicodemus had wondered, *Will God actually reveal Himself to His people during my lifetime?*

The teachings of Jesus had stirred his heart like nothing before and caused him to question, for the first time, some of the things he had been taught since childhood. He challenged them to believe in God's forgiveness through grace, an issue that angered his peers, as did Jesus' claims of Sonship to God. And then there was the subject of a spiritual new birth. On the surface and through eyes of human reasoning, it seemed preposterous. Yet, deep within his heart, Nicodemus knew there was truth within Jesus' words.

The people were naturally drawn to Jesus. The times Nicodemus thought of the most were the days when Jesus taught on the hillsides outside of Bethany. Just the thought of listening to Him tell of the kingdom of God and those who would live there was exciting and stirred Nicodemus's passionate side. What he would give to have those days back. Not even Joseph thought the envy and jealousy of a few spoiled temple officials would lead to this—not to the crucifixion of an innocent man.

Suddenly, a chilling cry broke through Nicodemus's thoughts. It was Jesus crying out, "*Eli, Eli, lama sabachthani?*" ("My God, My God, why have You forsaken Me?") These words sent a shiver through Nicodemus's body. How could God turn His back on Jesus? His entire life had been dedicated to telling of God's endless love for all of mankind. It made no sense.

Neither did the outcry of the people standing near the cross. Over and over again, the people who had cheered His arrival in Jerusalem the day before now mocked Him in death. They shouted for Jesus to come down from the cross and save Himself. Many laughed when they thought He called for Elijah, a dead prophet, to come and save Him.

Finally, in what appeared to be a dichotomy of victory and defeat, Jesus cried out once more and yielded up His spirit to heaven. Even as He had lived, Jesus' last words were a prayer of forgiveness for those who had crucified Him.

A few moments later a young soldier approached the base

of the cross with a spear in his hand. Joseph straightened and Nicodemus gasped, "But Joseph, He is already dead!"

"Yes, but there is evil in the air, Nicodemus. I must return to Pilate for the release of the body. We will have to hurry to complete the burial before the Sabbath begins." Joseph watched as John, one of the disciples closest to Jesus, comforted Mary, the Lord's mother. The anguish she suffered was heartwrenching. "We won't have an easy time of it," continued Joseph. "The women will certainly insist on following us."

Nicodemus was listening, yet his mind was active with the words of the prophets, Isaiah in particular. "He was pierced for our transgressions." "He was crushed for our iniquities."

"Joseph, could He have been . . . ?"

"The Messiah?" answered Joseph. "I don't know for sure. Yet I do know He was a man from God, maybe not the military man we had hoped would come. Still, He was God's choice, and that's all that matters."

"But, Joseph, to allow Him to die on a cross . . . like a common criminal? I tell you, it's too much for me to understand."

"And for me, Nicodemus. But remember His words the last time we spoke with Him. He said this very thing had to happen so that the words of the prophets would be fulfilled." Joseph reached out to touch his friend's shoulder. "So we must have courage even though we do not understand what we are seeing."

Nicodemus agreed. "I remember the night I found Him teaching under the olive trees outside the city. He spoke of

God giving His only Son to us as a sacrifice. He said if only I would believe. . . . I wanted to believe. My heart burned with truth, but my mind did not understand all that He was saying. Joseph, will I ever understand?"

"We must try, dear friend, but for now our hearts are too heavy. Later we will talk and ask God to help us to understand all that has happened. However, for now, stay close to the cross and watch over His body. I will return to the city for the parchment with Pilate's seal."

As Joseph hurried along the windswept street of Jerusalem, a cold, hard rain began to fall. His outer robe, heavy and wet, left him chilled and shivering. He had to return to the praetorium, the fatal scene of the previous night's illegal inquisition. Because it was so close to the temple walls, Joseph secretly prayed that he would avoid any trouble that might be waiting there for him.

As he turned the corner, he noticed a small group of temple officials gathered and gesturing frantically. He ducked in the alcove of a nearby building. From there he could hear most of what his former friends and teachers of the Law were discussing.

"I tell you," said Nathan, "I saw it with my own eyes. The curtain was torn from the top to the bottom! No man—only God—could accomplish something like this."

Joseph tried to lean closer to the conversation, but was afraid he would be seen. Something had happened other than Jesus' crucifixion, and whatever it was, it was monumental.

The usually calm and calculating Nathan was outraged.

"The people must not know. If they find out, they will say that this Jesus had something to do with it."

"Yes," said David. "They could easily claim it was the wrath of God. No one beyond us must know!"

Jonathan, a young student of the Law and one of Joseph's pupils, left the crowd and headed down the roadway. At one time he, too, had expressed an interest in Jesus as a teacher and rabbi, but he had never made an outward commitment. Mistakenly, Joseph felt safe in calling out to him. He forgot that the events of the day had immediately changed his status among temple rulers. From now on, both he and Nicodemus would be viewed as sympathizers to Jesus Christ. This alone was enough to cause other members of the Sanhedrin to challenge their membership on the council.

Fear of exposure was pushed aside. Joseph wanted to know what had happened in the temple to bring six men out into the streets in a fit of anxiety. "Jonathan!" called Joseph.

The young student turned and looked toward the corner of the line of buildings. He smiled slightly as he saw Joseph stepping away from the shadow of a small doorway.

"So, Joseph, you have already heard . . . and what of your friend Jesus? They say He is dead."

Joseph's "yes" was soft and almost undetectable. Then he asked, "What has happened?"

"I thought you knew. Why else would you be here?" The young man paused to study his teacher's face. "But what's the difference? You'll find out anyway. You have plenty of friends left on the council. Someone will tell you even if I don't. This afternoon, about the same time your teacher died, the curtain surrounding the Holy of Holies was torn from the ceiling to the floor!" Jonathan's eyes narrowed as he underscored a fact that Joseph had known since childhood. "No man has ever seen into the Holy of Holies except for the high priest on the Day of Atonement. But now it is open for everyone to see into the very throne room of God!"

Joseph's shock was evident. And his mind quickly returned to Jesus and the day He had spoken out against the chief priest and elders. Standing in the temple courtyard, He shouted, "My house shall be called a house of prayer; but you have made it a den of robbers." Then He challenged them by saying that if they tore the temple of God down to the ground, He would rebuild it within three days.

"No mere man died on that cross today," said Joseph. But his words fell on deaf ears as Jonathan's blank stare met his eyes. Without another word, his young pupil turned to go. And after a few paces he turned back, but only to shake his head in disgust.

Climbing the steps to the praetorium, Joseph felt physically sick. No decent Jew would ever do what he was doing, going to Pilot in this place. Caiaphas, during last night's mockery and arrest of Jesus, had sent others to do his bidding at the praetorium. And even they had refused to enter Pilot's place of refuge for fear of defilement.

Now he, Joseph of Arimathea, a once respected member of the Sanhedrin, was standing before the head of the praetorium guard waiting for the death certificate of a convicted criminal, a man whom he had loved and believed to be a teacher from God.

When Joseph returned, he found Nicodemus waiting near the cross.

"This will work," Joseph said as he approached his friend. "It has Pilate's seal on it. Jesus' body is ours to bury."

Noticeably out of breath, Joseph continued, "Nicodemus, there is something else. The curtain in the temple . . ."

"Yes?"

"It was torn."

"Torn? What are you saying? How could it be torn? It's too thick to be torn. You must be mistaken."

Nicodemus had stopped and was intently watching his friend. "No, I'm not. The temple leaders are saying that it happened at the time of Jesus' death."

Nicodemus shook his head in disbelief. "And what do you think they will tell the people?" His words turned sarcastic.

"They don't plan to say anything," answered Joseph.

"Exactly," countered Nicodemus. "And I tell you another thing, all of us will have to deal with Jesus' death one way or the other. This time there will be no escaping the judgment of God for an innocent man's death."

Joseph noticed the small group of women who had remained near the cross. They had been followers of Jesus, and they too wanted to help in His burial. Even though John and Mary had gone back to her home, these faithful few remained. Their frightened eyes told a story of disbelief and fear.

Joseph took a deep breath and sighed. "We had better get started if we plan to be done before the Sabbath begins."

Fear was leaving him. The more Joseph talked with the guards, the more he became aware of the need to deal quickly and swiftly with the situation. A lifetime of sorrows had filled this one day. Nothing could bring Jesus back, and it was certainly not the time to give in to fear.

Godly courage was all he had to rely on, and it was enough to help him approach the commander of these men. Joseph knew these men had been assigned to keep watch over Jesus' body. Pilot had made that clear. Yet within his hands was all the permission he and Nicodemus needed to perform one last act of love and friendship.

"We have permission to take the body." Joseph's words were firm. However, the commander was not impressed.

Nicodemus's eyes flushed with tears as he viewed the beaten and crucified body hanging limp on the cross. Jesus would be the first to be removed. The two other crucified men were dying a much slower death. And with the nearing of the Sabbath, the guards became anxious to end this ordeal. Jewish law demanded that the prisoners, if not dead, be removed from the crosses until the Sabbath was over. Usually the legs of the dying men were broken to hasten the process.

Suffocation comes quickly that way, thought Nicodemus as he watched the guards use brute strength and massive clubs to hasten the process. Suddenly an uncontrollable nausea swept over him as his mind fought the stench of death and hollow cries of dying men. He was grateful that Jesus was already dead and did not have to face this horror as well.

The commander cast an annoyed glance in Nicodemus's direction then looked back at Joseph. He unrolled the parchment and scanned the page. Pilate's seal was sufficient.

"The body's yours. That is, what is left of it," he said,

slapping the document back into Joseph's hand. "But tell me, what's a good Jew like you going to do with the body of a Jewish traitor? I thought you and those like you were the ones who put Him here in the first place?" The commander's words tore at Joseph's mind while the guards' laughter filled the air.

Raising the ladder to the back of the cross, Joseph grabbed the rope that would be used to lower the body and climbed until he reached the top of the cross. Looking out across the rocky landscape, he saw the city and realized that Jesus had died with Jerusalem in sight.

The quietness that accompanies death is always strange and foreboding. Death's finality can break even the strongest of hearts. Joseph had witnessed many deaths, but this one was different, this death had changed the way he viewed life.

The rope was looped around Jesus' chest and under His arms and then back up and over the beams of the cross. Once the nails were removed from the wrist and ankles, the body hung limp and was then lowered to the ground.

The guards offered no assistance as they watched Nicodemus and Joseph struggle with the lifeless form of their friend. If anything, they hampered the efforts with their jeering and complaints.

Finally, the body was covered, and they made their way away from the place known as "the skull" because of the many crucifixions that had taken place there. Suddenly, Joseph's grasp on the cloth gave way as he slipped in the mud. But at the same moment, a young guard stepped forward and steadied him.

He had not been with the others. His young face wore the

agony of what he had witnessed. "My son, were you near Him when He died?" asked Joseph.

The young man looked up and nodded. "Sir, He told me that He forgave me."

Joseph's voice cracked with emotion as he answered. "Yes, it is true. He has forgiven all of us."

The guard stepped out of their way but remained and watched as Joseph and Nicodemus continued down the rain-soaked incline. But the pain the guard was dealing with was too great for him to bear alone. He called out to them, "How can I learn more about this man who is called the Christ?"

Joseph smiled a painful smile. He knew it wasn't over. The work that Jesus had begun would continue. Death could not destroy Him.

"Find John and the other disciples," shouted Joseph. "They will show you the way!"

The place where Jesus was to be buried was only a short distance from Golgotha. Joseph's personal tomb would be Jesus' final resting place. At the time of its purchase, even Joseph had been hesitant about the tomb's location. Golgotha and the sounds accompanying crucifixion were so close. Now as he carried Jesus' body to the tomb, he wondered if some-how God had guided him in his decision.

The stresses and sadness of the day had left him and Nicodemus visibly shaken and somehow closer in friendship. Yet there was never a word between them concerning their newly established alliance. Some things are better left said in silence. And in this, their last gift to their friend and teacher, neither felt there were words adequate enough to express the emotions of their hearts.

Joel, Joseph's servant, met them as they approached the garden tomb. He had been instructed to guard the spices and yards of white linen that were to be used in the burial process.

Exhausted, Nicodemus and Joseph laid the body down and gathered their breath. Nicodemus cast a weary glance back at the women who had followed. His heart hurt for them, and for himself, and for all of mankind.

"Oh, Jesus," he whispered as he lifted the bloodstained covering away from the cut and bruised face of the Savior. Once it had been so full of life and compassion. He remembered Jesus' eyes and the acceptance he had found there, even for himself.

Sin was not a barrier to Him, thought Nicodemus. He recalled the tears and the shame of the woman caught in the act of adultery. The Pharisees had demanded her death by stoning. But did Jesus condemn her? No. Instead, He challenged the temple leaders to consider their own sin by saying, "Let those among you who are without sin cast the first stone." After they had gone, Jesus comforted the woman. No, He didn't dismiss her sinful lifestyle but told her to leave it behind and sin no more. It was hope and salvation that He offered, not condemnation and ridicule.

In fact, He never left anyone hopeless or floundering in despair. But did people understand His love, this gift of grace? *Obviously not,* thought Nicodemus. *They wanted judgment. Their hearts had grown hard and cold in the face of tradition. Their minds were stilted toward the Law, and while Jesus claimed to be the fulfillment of the Law, He certainly had a strange way of doing it.*

Joel was beside them now with a basin of water. Nothing more could be said. The task was before them, and both men would have to work feverishly to complete it before sunset.

Finally the last strip of cloth was secured, and Jesus was placed in the tomb. Nicodemus stepped through the doorway, wiped the sweat from his face, and looked down at his robe. It was stained with the Savior's blood. Suddenly, Christ's words came back to him, "You must be born again." It wasn't a physical rebirth Jesus spoke of but a spiritual one. But how . . . ?

Nicodemus's eyes returned to the women. They were still waiting and huddled together. Faithfully and tearfully, they had kept watch. Comfort was all he could offer them, but would they trust him? What did they think of him, a Jewish leader who had stood by and watched as others condemned and crucified their friend and Lord?

Mary Magdalene dismissed his fears when, looking up through tears of tenderness, she asked, "Sir, have you finished with our Lord?"

"Yes, Mary. All that we could do has been done." Nicodemus knew the women would try to come back after the Sabbath, but for the moment there was nothing more anyone could do. More soldiers were arriving. The two who had followed the procession from the crucifixion site had grown into a garrison.

"Mary, Jesus would not want you to remain here any longer. And I doubt that the guards will allow it. We must all go home. There is nothing more for us here."

The women agreed, but Mary insisted that she would return after the Sabbath to finish the burial process. Nicodemus didn't bother to tell her that he had given all the spices he owned for the burial. He realized that their expression of love and loyalty was very important.

Joseph stepped to the doorway of the tomb and looked back at the wrapped encasement. "Lord," he whispered, but the sound of the word still felt foreign to his lips. He was too tired to think. Instead he knew he had to find Nicodemus so they could seal the tomb.

A large, round stone waited to the left of the entranceway. Once the stops had been removed, it rolled down a hollowed-out groove before coming to an abrupt halt in front of the tomb opening. Both men stood for a moment, sensing the finality of the moment and not knowing what to do next.

They were not the only ones concerned about the protection of Jesus' body. Rome was very much interested in its care, as was evidenced by soldiers who immediately placed a Roman seal on the exterior of the tomb.

Joseph and Nicodemus took charge of their next task and made sure the women returned home safely. Once in front of her humble dwelling, Mary turned and asked, "Will you come back to us, Joseph? You are welcome here anytime, as is Nicodemus. Besides, you belong among us now."

Both men looked at one another. Their eyes showed their exhaustion. "My heart can take no more." Joseph sighed. "We will return in a couple of days, Mary. Maybe after the Sabbath has passed. Nicodemus and I have much to explain to Caiaphas and the others." Mary nodded as she entered the doorway to her house.

Alone on the street, Nicodemus instinctively rubbed his arms. "I'm chilled, and I'm fighting with being fearful, Joseph."

"I know, I feel it too," replied Joseph.

The last light of day was now filtering away. The grayness leftover from the rain was all around them. It was a lonely feeling. The kind of feeling that sinks deep within one's stomach. Joseph knew there would be very little either man could do to remove it or to change the impact of the day's events. Jesus Christ was dead, and nothing could change that.

The two parted—Nicodemus to his home and Joseph to his—ceremonially unclean and no longer the gallant, worldly Pharisees who had once dominated and held easy sway over their Sanhedrin peers. True, they would be remembered by some for their knowledge of the Law and Jewish tradition, but from this day forward, they were more likely to be remembered as sympathizers to a man who blasphemed Israel and proclaimed Himself to be the Son of God.

It was the third day after the crucifixion, and Joseph wondered if he would ever regain full consciousness. Mental exhaustion tried once again to reclaim his mind, and Joseph collapsed back into his bed. Somewhere in between sleep and consciousness, Joseph became aware of a sweet fragrance filling his room. It was so strong that he opened his eyes and sat up in bed and tried to understand where it was coming from. No one was with him. His wife's perfume certainly did not rival this. He could hear her downstairs going through the motions of the day.

The fragrance was like nothing he had ever smelled before. He rose and went to the window hoping some logical explanation would present itself there, but it didn't. Nothing seemed out of the ordinary except for the brilliance of the day.

Joseph thought of Jesus and the words He had spoken before His death. And though he didn't understand how, Joseph knew the Lord was connected with all he was feeling. He had to find Nicodemus; perhaps then he could get some answers.

By the time he rounded the corner to Nicodemus's house, it was late in the day. Change was in the air, but Joseph had no idea what kind of change was before him.

"Nicodemus!" he shouted as he opened the door without the customary knock. "Are you here, my friend?"

"Yes, Joseph! I am here," came the reply.

The sight facing Joseph as he entered the room nearest the kitchen area was tender. Nicodemus, obviously worn from lack of sleep, was kneeling beside his wife as they sang a Jewish song of peace.

As they concluded, Nicodemus looked up at Joseph with indescribable joy. "Have you heard?" asked Nicodemus.

"Heard what? I haven't left my house for two days."

"He is alive!" shouted Nicodemus.

"Who is?"

"Jesus! Mary saw Him this morning at the tomb. He instructed her to go and tell the others."

"Alive? That's nonsense." Joseph grabbed his head in his

hands as if to keep it from exploding and sat down in a nearby chair. "We were the ones that placed Him in the tomb, Nicodemus. We watched as the stone rolled in front of the grave opening. Remember? You were there! You saw the guard seal the tomb. Mary must be overwhelmed and out of her mind with grief."

Joseph stopped his rambling long enough to look into Nicodemus's eyes. "I tell you, Nicodemus, these past few days have certainly been more than I can handle."

"Joseph, Joseph, calm your heart. There is more you must hear. I went to the temple this morning, and yes, it is as we feared. Most think we have betrayed our commitment to Israel. Others, a few, thought it perfectly reasonable that we provided a Jewish burial for Him, since He was a Jew. But as I was leaving, there was such a sound and confusion among the people. There were reports from all over the city of loved ones being raised from the dead. I came home as quickly as possible, and we have been in prayer ever since."

The two men looked at one another. Both had the same thought at the same time—Mary! They had to find Mary and learn for sure if it was true. Had she seen Jesus, and if so, where was He now?

The day was steadily drawing to an end. Joseph's heart pounded as he hurried to keep one step in front of Nicodemus's long and arching stride. Was it true? Was Jesus really alive? How could it be? He had wound the cloth around the lifeless form with his own hands and watched as the mammoth stone fell into place. How could it be?

They tried several houses but found no one home. One

place remained, the home of Mary, Jesus' mother. Out of respect, Joseph deliberately saved it until last. He thought surely they would have found someone before coming to her home, but none of the disciples or women had been seen since earlier in the day.

Joseph knocked, but there was no reply. He lifted the handle on the door, and the darkness of the entranceway engulfed him. No one was home. This was their last hope for the evening. And in hopelessness, he fought to hold back the feelings of fear and frustration welling up inside of him.

Mary and the women were not there to comfort their anxious minds. For Joseph, it was the final block atop a tumbling wall of pent-up emotion. "Alone!" he shouted as his fist sailed through the darkness, seeking something to receive its blow. "I'm alone!" came his second shout.

"Joseph!" shouted Nicodemus as he pulled his friend back out into the evening air. There was a struggle and both men went down to the ground. Their shouts and sobs ceased as they felt the presence of someone near them.

Nicodemus turned quickly to the left but saw no one. He started to stand as his eyes caught sight of the approaching figure. It was huge. Joseph tried to speak but something gripped his tongue. With one powerful stride, the stranger stepped forward and a burst of light radiated out from around him.

The force of his presence sent both men back against the wall of the house. Joseph sank to his knees and Nicodemus followed. A voice blazed through their minds and penetrated the depths of their hearts.

"A messenger from God," gasped Joseph as he fell forward.

"Men called of God. Why are your hearts troubled? Have you not heard? The same Jesus that you laid to rest in the garden tomb is alive and now among you. He has risen to His God and your God, His heavenly Father and your heavenly Father. Go in peace. The Lord is faithful. He abides with His people forever!"

Just as quickly as it had appeared, the brilliant light withdrew, and the figure disappeared. For a moment neither man moved or spoke. Finally, gathering themselves together, they stood.

"Joseph, it's true!" Nicodemus's eyes twinkled with joyous laughter. "Jesus is alive! Jesus is alive. We don't have to be afraid!"

"Yes!" shouted Joseph, smiling and raising his hands toward heaven. "Yes! He's alive, and the kingdom of God truly has come to us!"

He turned and ran out into the city street.

"Joseph, where are you going?" shouted Nicodemus.

"To the building and the room where Jesus was with His disciples the night of His arrest. I want to find John and Peter and James and the others."

"But why?"

Joseph stopped for a moment and looked at his friend. "Mary was right, Nicodemus. I belong with them now. Jesus has changed me, and I will never be the same. I have been touched by His love, and I must go there. If I am ever to see Him again, I know I must be with the others."

Nicodemus paused for a moment and then ran to catch up with his friend. "It's my commitment, too, Joseph. I want to go and know for myself this life and the way of Jesus Christ."

The two men smiled, embraced, and together stepped back into the darkness of the night, a darkness that had been shattered and had lost its power by the light of God's love forevermore.

A WINDOW TO GOD'S HEART

Joseph and Nicodemus were men of commitment. They had long since tossed aside the notion of ease and pleasure. They were guardians of the Law of Moses, educators of Jewish tradition, the lamplighters of God's truth. They were also men of spiritual ambition and pride. No matter how you sliced the message of their lives, Jewish piety was their crowning glory. But something happened to them once they met Jesus Christ. The picture is not very clear and often open to debate. The apostle John calls Joseph a secret follower of the Lord, and Nicodemus will forever remain the one who came to the Master by night.

No one knows exactly how the two men first heard of Jesus. Perhaps through the words of a friend, the testimony of someone healed by His touch, or they simply may have heard Jesus speaking in a local synagogue. One thing is certain, as Pharisees and members of the Sanhedrin, they kept up with His day-to-day journeys, watching for a time when they could personally examine the content of His message.

While Joseph may have accepted Jesus as being a man sent

from God, Nicodemus needed more evidence. Indeed, he did go to Jesus under the cover of night's darkness; perhaps it was out of fear of being seen by his peers who would demand an explanation for his actions. By the end of John's gospel, Nicodemus's commitment was no longer a mystery. No one helps to bury a crucified man without having befriended him in some way.

Commitment is often a hard command.

From a human perspective, Nicodemus and Joseph had far more to lose than the local fishermen Jesus called to follow Him, but this is not so. Each of us must answer the same call to follow Christ regardless of social status or occupation.

Neither Joseph's nor Nicodemus's name appears in any of the Jewish records from this period of time. Some scholars believe they are legendary figures. But somehow this seems doubtful, given the eyewitness account of John's writings and his closeness with Jesus. A reasonable deduction is that once they completed the burial process and returned to their homes, they were renounced by other Jewish leaders, and their names were stricken from the records.

Commitment will always cost you something.

It cost Jesus His life at Calvary, and it may cost you something that seems very significant. The rich young ruler wanted to follow Jesus but could not forsake his desire for wealth. The issue was not how much he had, because often God blesses us materially. Instead it involves the focus of our hearts. The thing that captivates a person's life ultimately will rule it.

Commitment always involves choice.

At some point, Nicodemus and Joseph had to make a choice to follow Jesus. The fact that they waited until His death is not discouraging. At least they gathered their courage and offered God all that was within their power to give and, in doing so, chose to follow when others had gone into hiding.

Commitment to Jesus Christ is a lifelong adventure.

There are times in our walk with Christ when God challenges, strengthens, and renews our commitment. By the time the cross had been lifted into place at Calvary, Joseph's quiet commitment had matured into a bold confession of faith.

God calls each of us to a firm commitment to His Son through faith. Once we make that commitment, we are freed to live above the pain and brokenness of a sin-torn society. This doesn't mean that we will never face hardships and trials. It means that when they do come, we have Someone living within us who is stronger and more powerful than the deepest and darkest adversity.

In commitment we gain the victory . . . *forevermore!*

CHAPTER 7

Window of Hope—*The Road to Emmaus*

"If only they would follow the truth instead of their human emotions," said Araius, his eyebrow raised slightly.

"Yes," replied Ephron while shaking his head somewhat in frustration.

"But the Lord is merciful. They will be given yet another chance!"

Araius looked down from his heavenly post to the solitary travelers and smiled at Ephron. "In fact, they all will. Calvary was just the beginning."

The two ageless creatures instinctively lifted their right arms in a victory shout. "To God be the glory, forever!"

Ephron added, "This is the reason we guard them until redemption's plan has been revealed to them."

From above, they watched the lone disciples make their way along the rut-filled road to Emmaus. Suddenly, the two forlorn human travelers were no longer alone as a third companion appeared behind them.

Ephron turned quickly to Araius as a brilliant, white light swept over the two travelers. In unison, the angels bowed in worship. A symphony of praise rang out through the heavens announcing the presence of the risen Lord.

"They are safe now," whispered Araius. "We must return to Jerusalem. There is still so much to do." Disappearing through the clouds with the speed of lightning, the two spiritual beings became flashes of light against the backdrop of the afternoon sky.

The week's events had taken their toll on Cleopas. For the first time in a long time he knew what it meant to feel hopeless and defeated. Yet his friend Phillip rambled on endlessly about Jesus and the events of the past week. It was as if he hoped to undo all that had happened. Cleopas tried to stay focused on his friend's words, but it was no use. His mind wandered.

Even the warmth of the setting sun could not break the icy chill clinging to his emotions. Surely they hadn't been deceived by the man who claimed to be God's Son? If Jesus was an impostor, wouldn't they have felt it in their hearts?

"I tell you, Cleopas, there is something strange in all of this. I mean, the stone was rolled away from the tomb. How . . . Cleopas! . . . Are you listening?"

Cleopas blinked as he turned to his friend. Phillip had stopped in midsentence.

A lonely smile embraced his face. "Sorry," said Cleopas. "I guess I wasn't with you. I was somewhere back on a Galilean hillside thinking through the words of Jesus and the things He spoke of so very often."

"Do you remember the time He sent us to Judea to tell of His coming?"

"Do I? There were seventy of us. We were so young in our beliefs and so sincere in our desire to follow Him."

Phillip shook his head in amazement at the memory. "We were wild with excitement. I remember He told us not to rejoice over the fact that the spirits fell in subjection to us. But instead, we should rejoice over the fact that our names were recorded in heaven."

Looking down and then back up at Cleopas, Phillip's eyes narrowed. "Our names are in heaven," he echoed. "How will we ever know for sure now that He is . . ."

"Greetings!" came the call from behind them. Turning around, they saw a tall, dark-complexioned man standing across the roadway.

Amazingly, His presence did not shock or frighten them. "You men look as if you could use some company. I know it would make My journey more enjoyable. May I join you?"

Etched out in the final refrain of the day's sunlight, the Stranger's face glowed with an inviting warmth. It bore a strength and a sureness that was stunning. Even His deeply set eyes seemed to exude an unexplainable joy. Cleopas hesitated, then looked at Phillip. Neither had noticed Him before this moment. Where had He come from?

Cleopas nodded hesitantly while offering the explanation. "We may not be the best company."

"Oh, really?" the Stranger was now at their side. "Just a moment ago, I know I saw an eagerness on your faces."

"The eagerness we shared was for a faded dream," said Cleopas.

"A hope once shared by many people," echoed Phillip sadly.

"A faded dream? A hope once shared and now seemingly gone?" asked the Stranger.

"Yes, surely You have heard of the events in Jerusalem?" Cleopas tried not to appear impatient.

The Stranger winced and for a moment seemed to be deep in thought. "Tell Me, what were you talking about as you walked along the road? Surely, you were not just engrossed in sadness?"

But their sorrow was all too apparent. The memory too fresh, too painful. Neither wanted to speak, and for the moment, the question seemed like a horrible joke. Did He really not know what had happened, or was He making light of the situation?

"Are you the only One traveling through Judea who is unaware of all that has taken place over the past three days?" asked Cleopas.

"What things are you talking about?" He said, appearing ignorant of the events of the past three days.

Cleopas and Phillip were shocked. "The crucifixion of the Nazarene, Jesus Christ," snapped Cleopas. "Many believed He was a prophet from God."

Phillip joined the assault. "People came from miles around to hear Him teach. He was truly a mighty man of God, but the chief priests and rulers could not accept this. So they sought

His arrest and crucifixion. He died a horrible death on a Roman cross for something He did not do."

Cleopas nodded. "They accused Him of treason, but that was not the issue. It was the Pharisees' anger and jealousy that nailed Him to the cross."

"It was their fear," Phillip chimed in. "Pilate was but a pawn in their hands and thus condemned an innocent man to die. For the sake of peace, he caved in to their pressure and ordered Jesus crucified. Now that He is dead, any hope of redemption is dead as well."

Cleopas's eyes dropped. "Those of us who followed Him thought He was the One the prophets spoke of—the Messiah—the One sent from God to redeem Israel. There is nothing left for us to do but return home and try somehow to get on with our lives. Yet, there is one strange aspect to Jesus' death. Phillip, you were with some of the disciples this morning. Tell Him about the women and what they saw at the tomb."

As the men walked toward their hometown of Emmaus, Cleopas described how the women who had followed Jesus had gone to His tomb early that morning after the Sabbath had come to an official end.

"They had hoped to complete the burial process by adding fresh spices to the body. However, when they arrived, the tomb was open, and the body was gone. Suddenly, two men stood near them in dazzling apparel and said, 'Why do you seek the living among the dead? Jesus is not here but has risen.'

"The women were frightened and bowed down, thinking

these men were angels from God. They told the women to think back on the words of Jesus, how when He was in Galilee He told us that He must be delivered into the hands of sinful men and be crucified. Yet, on the third day, He would rise again.

"The women ran to tell John and Peter, but Mary Magdalene stayed behind. It was then that Jesus appeared to her telling her not to be afraid and that it was true, He was alive. He instructed her to go to His disciples and tell them that He would meet with them very soon."

The Stranger took a deep breath. They had remembered that day in Galilee when He had tried to prepare them for His death and resurrection, but did they believe? "Do you believe the words He shared with you concerning His resurrection?"

"Our hearts burned with excitement and joy each time He spoke to us," said Cleopas. "Oh, there were times, as with any teacher, when the lessons seemed hard to comprehend. But the way He explained the words of the prophets brought hope and newness to our lives. Especially when He read from Isaiah. It was as if He knew him personally."

Phillip added, "We knew His words were truth. Our hearts identified with His message."

"Then you believe He was who He said He was," the Stranger asked, "the Son of God—the Messiah?"

The three stopped walking. Phillip and Cleopas looked down at the ground. "I don't know what I believe anymore," said Cleopas. "I know at the moment I would have given almost anything to stop His crucifixion. Now I'm so confused, I don't know what is true."

The Stranger turned to Phillip, who nodded in agreement, then He lifted His eyes to heaven. When He turned back to them, a sense of power radiated from His face.

"O foolish men and slow of heart to believe in all that the prophets have spoken! Was it not necessary for the Christ to suffer these things and to enter into His glory?"

Cleopas felt his breath leave his chest as a strong wind enveloped him. He tried to turn to Phillip, but the words of the prophets filled his mind in rapid succession.

Beginning with Moses, the Stranger conveyed all things concerning Jesus in the Scriptures.

Thirsty and needing to be filled, their minds drank from the fountain of truth. And their hearts burned with God's calling and the fulfilling of His prophecy. Still, they did not know that it was Jesus who was speaking to them.

Exhausted, Cleopas and Phillip collapsed to their knees on the roadside outside the city.

Cleopas was the first to break the silence. "We don't even know Your name. Yet Your words have touched our hearts with the deepest of meaning and emotion. My friend, I am far too weary to make sense out of all You have told us. Go with us a little farther. My house is only a short distance away, and I'm sure my wife has prepared an evening meal. Your company at my table would be most honored."

The Stranger's gaze saddened at the lack of their understanding. "I really need to continue My journey."

"Yes, but it is late and not safe to travel alone after dark," Phillip said, hoping the Stranger would change His mind.

Seeing the loneliness in their eyes and knowing the frailty

of their humanity, He agreed. "Very well, we will share the evening meal together."

Cleopas and Phillip smiled. "And You can continue to tell us of the prophecies of Isaiah," said Cleopas. "There is one point I always wanted to discuss with Jesus."

"I know exactly what you are going to ask," said Phillip while giving his friend an encouraging pat on the shoulder.

A joy filled Cleopas's heart as his wife opened the door to their home. Ruth had heard them enter the courtyard and hurried to meet them. Her eyes told the story—she, too, had heard what had happened in Jerusalem. Yet, because of their guests, Cleopas tried to calm her and reassure her that they would talk later.

The table was already prepared, as if she had known all along that Cleopas would return with guests for the evening meal.

After greeting the men, Ruth, who could stand it no longer, said, "The reports say Jesus did not even answer the accusations raised against Him! We also heard He died the death of a common criminal."

"It is true," said Cleopas, casting a look of caution in her direction. He understood her inability to keep her thoughts to herself, but for now, their guests must come first, especially the Stranger who was watching them with eyes of intensity.

Ruth sensed the tension and stepped out to the oven where the loaves of fresh barley bread were waiting. She filled a basket and delivered it to the men. Cleopas poured the wine and stepped back to admire the table. The meal was perfect.

Though they had a modest income, Ruth always made him

feel as if he were sitting down to a rich man's banquet. He never understood how she accomplished so much with so little.

Seeing her face tonight was a special blessing. The trials of the last three days had seemed, at times, to be overwhelming. Even the trip home was curiously exhausting. He needed to sense her love and devotion. A loneliness pulled at his heart from all that he had seen.

Almost three years before, he had witnessed the birth of a dream in the teachings of a young Jewish rabbi—a dream he had felt would change the course of Israel's future. Three days ago, he had witnessed the end of that dream with the death of Jesus Christ. Now he and his wife would have to start again. Somehow they would find the energy to pray and fast for Messiah's arrival.

Phillip was hungry and without thinking reached to grab a hot loaf of bread. Cleopas pointed out that it had not been properly blessed. The Stranger nodded to both men as He instinctively picked up the bread.

Holding it upward toward heaven, He prayed: "Father, bless this food and use it to nourish these bodies that these men may be witnesses of Your life in Me now and forever. Amen."

He tore the bread in half and, with arms outstretched, offered it to them. Immediately their eyes were opened as they saw the hands and wrists that bore the marks of crucifixion. But before either could speak, a blinding burst of white light filled the room, permeating their hearts and minds with the Word of God. The Messiah, the Son of God, was with them!

Cleopas dropped to the floor as Phillip fell back against the wall shouting, "Jesus! My Lord and my God!" He reached out to touch Him, but Christ vanished from before him.

Scrambling to his side, Cleopas, almost choking, joined Phillip. "It's the Lord! It was Jesus that walked with us on the road! My heart burned within me as He spoke of the prophets and told how all of this had to happen so that prophecy would be fulfilled! But I had no idea. . . . I have seen the risen Lord. Cleopas, it happened just as He said it would! Oh, why did we ever doubt?"

Cleopas reached for the piece of bread that Jesus had blessed and held it up to his friend. His eyes glowed with excitement. "It's not over. Nothing is over! It's only just begun! And we must go back to Jerusalem to tell the others. Jesus is alive! Alive forever!"

A WINDOW TO GOD'S HEART

Jesus told His disciples on several occasions that He would never leave them. His words were explicit. He would have to die, but He would return to them. Yet on the night of His arrest, fear and panic gripped their hearts, and they wondered what they would do next. Those who had remained faithfully at His side went into hiding. Only John and a reluctant Peter followed to see where the soldiers would take their Lord.

That night must have been very dark and lonely for the disciples. They had left everything, homes and often families, to follow Jesus. Now they had nothing, not even the comfort of His presence. Hopelessness and thoughts of abandonment tugged at their hearts. But when they were just about to give up, Jesus came to them.

A. B. Simpson once wrote, "When God tests you, it is a good time for you to test Him by putting His promises to the proof, and claiming from Him just as much as your trials have rendered necessary."† There are three easy steps to trusting God in difficult circumstances.

Recall the goodness of God and His past blessings.

After the eyes of the Emmaus disciples were opened, they realized they had been with Jesus. Immediately they began recalling what it felt like to be in His presence. "Did not our heart burn within us while He talked . . . ?" (Luke 24:32). When you face disappointment, one of your best defenses is to immediately recall God's past blessings. Jesus is your Advocate before the Father (1 John 2:1). David wrote, "Preserve me, O God, for in You I put my trust. / O my soul, you have said to the LORD, / 'You are my Lord, / My goodness is nothing apart from You.' . . . I will bless the LORD who has given me counsel; / My heart also instructs me in the night seasons. / I have set the LORD always before me; / Because He is at my right hand I shall not be moved" (Ps. 16:1–2; 7–8). Call out to Him. Ask Him to encourage your heart by helping you to remember the times He has provided for you in the past.

Renew your mind with God's Word.

Hopelessness is one of Satan's favorite tools. He knows that if he can discourage you, there's a strong chance you will give up and quit. However, you can change this by studying God's Word, not just laboring to memorize it but by asking God to show you how to apply His principles to your life. The men and women of the Bible were no different from any of us. They had problems, faced fears, and were called to believe God by faith. Pray for God to teach you how to apply His Word to every area of your life.

Recognize the victory that is yours in Christ.

In order for the principles of God to be yours, you must use them. This means when testing comes, you turn to Him and trust Him to help you through the hard times. Claim the promises of His Word. Ask Him to show you specific examples of others who have trusted and received His blessing.

Remember, the victory is yours. Even before His death, Jesus knew His disciples would go through a dark and lonely time. He also knew that He would return to them and remain with them forever. Through His resurrection, He once and for all broke the power of sin and death. We have the victory because we are not alone. The Son of God is alive within each believer.

When you face heartache, He is there to face it with you. When doubts creep in, He is our constant Encourager. And when fear tries to steal your joy, Jesus remains steadfast, true, and devoted to you. He is our hope in times of hopelessness, and in Him we have eternal victory.

† Mrs. Charles E. Cowman, *Streams in the Desert* (Grand Rapids, MI: Zondervan, 1980), 263.

About the Author

Angela Ramage is the editor of *In Touch* magazine, a monthly publication of IN TOUCH MINISTRIES®, the teaching ministry of Dr. Charles Stanley.

A graduate of Toccoa Falls College in Georgia, Angela majored in Christian Counseling. She stayed on at Toccoa Falls after graduation as director of public information, a position she had helped to establish during her years as a student there. She also edited the monthly alumni magazine and worked for the Stephens County mental health facility in Toccoa.

Before coming to IN TOUCH MINISTRIES® in 1990, Angela was an editor for Walk Thru the Bible Ministries. While at Walk Thru the Bible Ministries, she worked for the client services team, an editorial clearinghouse for Coral Ridge Ministries, Biola University, and Ligonier Ministries, among others. In addition to her editing responsiblities at *In Touch* magazine, Angela helps to write the articles and daily devotionals taken from Dr. Stanley's weekly sermons.

Windows to the Heart of God is Angela's first book.

DATE DUE